Spir

from Hinduism

Swami Mukundananda is a world-renowned spiritual teacher from India, an international authority on mind management, and a bestselling author who earned his degrees from the prestigious IIT Delhi and IIM Calcutta. He worked with a multinational firm for a short while before renouncing a promising career to enter monkhood. He studied the Vedic scriptures at the feet of Jagadguru Kripaluji Maharaj. For almost four decades now, he has been sharing his vast knowledge through his books, lectures, and life-transformation lectures.

Every day, Swamiji meets hundreds, and even thousands, of people from all walks of life. His steadfast positivity exudes hope, clarity, and a sense of purpose to those who connect with him. He has deeply affected the lives of millions of people who have been drawn by his profound integrity, charismatic personality, and passion to serve. Despite his hectic schedule, those who encounter him experience his warmth and compassion and feel deeply touched by him. Swamiji's lectures are humorous, his arguments are logical and well-laid out, and, most of all, his advice is practical. His lectures on social media platforms are loved and followed by millions. Swamiji divides his time between India and the US.

swamimukundananda.org
facebook.com/Swami.Mukundananda
instagram.com/Swami_Mukundananda
linkedin.com/in/swamimukundananda
twitter.com/Sw_Mukundananda
youtube.com/c/swamimukundananda

Other Books by the Author

7 Divine Laws to Awaken Your Best Self
(Also available in Hindi)

7 Mindsets for Success, Happiness and Fulfilment
(Also available in Hindi, Gujarati, Marathi, Oriya & Telugu)

Bhagavad Gita: The Song of God

Golden Rules for Living Your Best Life

Questions You Always Wanted to Ask

Science of Healthy Diet

Spiritual Dialectics

The Art & Science of Happiness

The Power of Thoughts

The Science of Mind Management
(Also available in Gujarati & Telugu)

Yoga for the Body, Mind & Soul

Books for Children

Essence of Hinduism

Festivals of India

Healthy Body Healthy Mind: Yoga for Children

Inspiring Stories for Children (set of 4 books)

Mahabharat: The Story of Virtue and Dharma

My Best Friend Krishna

My Wisdom Book: Everyday Shlokas, Mantras, Bhajans and More

Ramayan: The Immortal Story of Duty and Devotion

Saints of India

Praise for the Book

Sanatana dharma is eternal dharma, dharma that has spread for an eternity. The message of Hindutva is universal, unconstrained by a specific text and dogma. But precisely because it doesn't have a specific text, Hinduism's spiritual message is difficult to understand and imbibe. Who better than Swami Mukundananda, with his reader-friendly style, peppered with anecdotes and wit, to convey and communicate that template of dharma? A person who reads this book, and practices what it talks about, will become a better individual and make the world a better place.

—**Dr Bibek Debroy**, chairman, Economic Advisory Council to the Prime Minister of India

This latest book is a masterpiece that delves deep into the intricacies of spirituality and self-discovery, offering a profound exploration of Hinduism's core teachings and philosophies in a very simple and easy to understand format. Through its captivating storytelling and profound wisdom, the book felt like a guiding light, offering me both solace and inspiration. I highly recommend this book to anyone seeking a deeper connection to themselves and the Divine.

—**Dr R.R. Sudhir**, senior consultant and head, Department of Preventive Ophthalmology, Sankara Nethralaya, Medical and Vision Research Foundation, Chennai

If you are looking for clarity in your life and want to grow in your life, this book will take you step by step. This book is not just about spiritual growth and self-realization. Swamiji shares very useful insights from the Vedas in lucid language. A must-read for people of all ages.

—**Sweta Samota**, author and India's leading book coach

Drawing upon the Hindu scriptures, Swami Mukundananda takes the reader on a spiritual odyssey that brings clarity and direction to seekers. Swamiji's hospitable vision invites the novice as well as the seasoned spiritual traveller on a journey inward that resonates equally with both. The style of delivery appeals for its logical directness and succinct messaging. In his wisely conveyed guidance, he addresses questions that commonly arise in the minds of the spiritually curious. Connectivity with readers is enhanced by using relatable examples to deconstruct complex issues. This is a remarkable book that inspires reflection and a revisitation of one's assumptions about inner evolution. I recommend it highly to those embarking on this path of spiritual growth.

—**Dr Prakash Mirchandani**, professor and academic director, Executive MBA Program, Katz Graduate School of Business, University of Pittsburgh

Spirituality always elicits different meanings for different people. We experience a variety of scenarios on a daily basis that pose challenges to which we don't have ready solutions. However, over a course of time, we realize how those solutions lie within us, in the realm of our spiritual existence. *Spiritual Secrets from Hinduism* by His Holiness Swami Mukundananda is a key to that realm of spirituality where all the answers reside. Swamiji has laid out the framework of life in the simplest way possible through his book. Whether it is the path to karma or the secrets of the mind and the brain, his words are timeless. I truly feel that this book is the first step to understanding our connection to God, which in turn, will provide the clarity that many of us seek for ages.

—**Gaurav Shekhar**, senior assistant dean, Naveen Jindal School of Management, The University of Texas at Dallas

Once again, Swami Mukundananda has shed light on an often misunderstood area—ancient Vedic scriptures. His advice is at once both practical and profound e.g. ways to understand and reduce anger and greed, and tools for meditation and peace of mind.

One cannot go far in India without being aware of the strong impact of Swamiji's presence—whether it be his bestselling books at airports or posters of his upcoming talks. He leads spiritual retreats and has delivered transformational talks all over the world (Google, Microsoft, MIT, to name a few).

Thank you for all that you do, Swamiji, to make our lives more meaningful and purpose driven. I can't wait to learn even more from your latest book, which translates teachings from Vedas and other ancient knowledge sources to language for the modern world.

—**Debjani Biswas**, international bestselling author,
popular TEDx and global keynote speaker

Spiritual Secrets from Hinduism by Swami Mukundananda is a go-to book that masterfully distills spiritual concepts into clear, modern-day examples and analogies. It beautifully summarizes the essence of all scriptures, especially the Vedas, presenting complex philosophical ideas in a logical and easily understandable manner. Swamiji's ability to simplify profound teachings makes this book a must-read for anyone seeking to deepen their understanding of spirituality.

—**Dr Vineet Aggarwal**, bestselling author,
speaker, doctor, and blogger

Spiritual Secrets from Hinduism is an in-depth study of Vedic scriptures that illuminates the spiritual essence to reveal the complex contours of Hinduism for a diverse audience. It presents the profound wisdom of the Vedas in a very elegant manner, blending practical advice with philosophical depth. Swamiji, a highly respected spiritual teacher with an amazing academic background, explores the nature of the self, life's purpose, and the journey to God-realization in a structured manner that promotes progressive reading.

The book offers profound insights into Sanatan Dharma (Eternal Religion) by focussing on the quest for divine bliss and understanding the soul's eternal nature. Swamiji elaborates on the soul's journey, the critical role of self-effort, and the importance of surrendering to God, using very engaging examples. It guides readers through managing the mind, the importance of selfless love, and the practice of meditation, merging scriptural teachings with practical applications.

Spiritual Secrets from Hinduism serves as a guiding light for those seeking to enrich their lives with spiritual wisdom. Its uniqueness lies in its ability to demystify complex Vedic philosophy while retaining its depth and fostering a connection with the divine. Swamiji's work transcends the conventional notion of a book, acting as a mentor and guide on the spiritual path. It promises to awaken the Inner Self, inspire, and direct seekers towards self-realization and divine love.

—**Dr Ashutosh Garg**, CEO, coach, and founder, 'The Brand Called You' and Guardian Pharmacy

Spiritual Secrets *from* Hinduism

Essence of the Vedic Scriptures

Swami Mukundananda

RUPA

Published by
Rupa Publications India Pvt. Ltd 2024
7/16, Ansari Road, Daryaganj
New Delhi 110002

Sales centres:
Bengaluru Chennai
Hyderabad Jaipur Kathmandu
Kolkata Mumbai Prayagraj

P-ISBN: 978-93-6156-262-4
E-ISBN: 978-93-6156-630-1

Third impression 2024

10 9 8 7 6 5 4 3

Printed in India

This book is dedicated to my beloved Spiritual Master, Jagadguru Shree Kripaluji Maharaj, who illuminated this world with the purest rays of divine knowledge and devotion. He taught us by His example, the importance of nurturing souls with love and care, to help them realize a glorious future. He gave us the supreme process of building a noble value system by teaching selfless divine love. I am confident that by His blessings, this book will be helpful in inspiring and elevating seekers, thereby creating a better world for all of us.

Contents

Introduction

The human form we possess is a tremendous opportunity bestowed upon us to know the Absolute Truth. We must use it to attain the perfection our soul has been seeking since eternity. Reaching this supreme goal requires the highest profound knowledge. Such learning, which is pure and divine, is the key to elevating our life to sublime heights.

The Vedic scriptures are a vast treasure house of sacred wisdom. All over the world, seekers intuitively perceive Bharat as the land of spirituality. In the bosom of its heritage are the rarest of rare secrets that were known to sages who possessed the highest realizations. As such there exists an inherent curiosity to understand the concepts of Hinduism, read its scriptures, and visit the country that is the spiritual leader of the world.

However, without proper guidance, such endeavours to fathom the teachings of Hinduism do not succeed, despite the best of intentions. People get stumped about how to access the knowledge, grasp its wide spectrum of concepts, and utilize it meaningfully in their life. This is why Hinduism remains an enigma for most Westerners. Their clichéd understanding of Hinduism as a way of life does not even come close to the precious jewels in its repository.

Interestingly, Hinduism is not mentioned by this name anywhere in the Vedic scriptures. The word 'Hindu' was first coined by the Arabs to refer to the people who lived on the other side of the Indus River (called Sindhu in Sanskrit). This gave rise to the word 'Al-Hind' for the land across Indus, and the name of the religion they practised became adopted in English as 'Hinduism'. Over time, the word 'Hinduism' has acquired other connotations. It has come to represent the values, beliefs, and religious practices that have originated from the Vedic scriptures.

The Vedas, however, have a very different and majestic perspective on the nomenclature of their teachings. The Vedas are the eternal knowledge of God, and hence, the religion described in them is called Sanatan Dharma, or the 'Eternal Religion'. It is the path to the Supreme realization, based on scientific, non-sectarian, and eternal principles.

This book has been written with the goal of teaching the perennial principles of Sanatan Dharma. Keeping this in mind, the wisdom of the Vedic scriptures has been distilled and presented to make it comprehensible to everyone—including Westerners and youth. At the same time, key concepts have been explained with philosophic depth for the satisfaction of the more erudite readers. Along with relevant verses from the sacred books, practical examples have been included for demonstrating their relevance to everyday life.

Topics have been sequentially arranged, enabling readers to

reconcile the subject matter of numerous Vedic scriptures in one place. They are based on Jagadguru Shree Kripaluji Maharaj's *Prema Rasa Siddhanta.* Since the chapters follow a logical flow, it is recommended that they be read in the same sequence.

I sincerely pray that *Spiritual Secrets from Hinduism: Essence of the Vedic Scriptures* will illuminate your intellect, touch your heart, and nourish your soul as you repeatedly turn to it for spiritual succour.

1

Nature of the Self

The spiritual quest begins with an inquiry into the nature of the self. 'Who am I?' This question has captured the interest of several profound thinkers throughout history. The awareness of 'I' remains with us at all times. For example, 'I am reading', 'I am eating', 'I am walking', and so on. However, what is this 'I' we are referring to? It is a mystery for most people.

When you look at your family album, you see the picture of a newborn baby, and say, 'That is me'. Then you find the picture of a two-year old, and say, 'That is also me'. Then there is a picture of a five-year old, and you say, 'That is me too'. Now, who are you?

The body is continuously changing. If you were the body, you too would have changed. However, you intuitively realize you are the same person who was the newborn baby, then the two-year old, and then the five-year old.

Biology informs us that the human body consists of trillions of cells. These cells die, and new ones are created in their place.

The process of regeneration changes the entire body every seven years. And yet, despite the constantly changing body, we remain the same person.

We learn from the Vedas that within the body is the unchanging atma (soul). It is the real 'I', the true self. The body is material, while the atma is divine, just as God is divine. And, like God, the soul is immortal as well.

At this point, some ask, 'What is the proof for the existence of this divine entity within our body?'

Consciousness—Evidence of the Soul

Is it possible to close your eyes, and read this book with your nose? Definitely not! The nose cannot see; the eyes cannot smell. All the senses have limited purviews. If we wish to read, we must use our eyes.

Likewise, our senses are material, while our soul is divine; it cannot be perceived by the senses, no matter how hard we try. With this limitation, what is the evidence of the soul's existence? The most compelling evidence is consciousness—presence of life in the body.

All matter is lifeless, and our body is made from matter. Hence, the body by itself cannot be the reason for life. Science realizes this paradox and is grappling to explain the phenomenon of consciousness. If matter could be manipulated to create consciousness, then scientists would do the same in laboratories. However, nobody has ever succeeded in creating life from matter. Philosophers, therefore, continue to debate over the origin of consciousness.

The Vedas explain that 'life', or sentience, originates from the soul. As long as the atma is present in the body, the brain, heart, kidneys, and liver continue to work. Once it departs, the organs are still there, but all functions cease. The body is now deemed 'dead'. Hence, consciousness, or 'life', comes from the soul.

Here, a question may arise: How does the soul give life to the body? The *Brahma Sutra* explains: *vyaktireko gandhanvat* (2.3.26) 'A flower is inherently fragrant. When it grows in a garden, it also makes the garden aromatic by its presence.' Likewise, the soul possesses life, and when present, it makes the dead matter of the body come alive as well.

Location of the Soul

In the body, where does the atma reside? The *Prashnopanishad* answers: *hṛidi hyeṣha ātmā* (3.6) 'The soul is situated in the heart.'

But this does not mean it is physically locked to the heart. During a cardiac transplant, the soul continues to reside in the heart region of the body, even when the physical organ is removed.

This leads to the next question. If the soul stays only in one place—the heart—how does it make the entire body alive? Again, the *Brahma Sutra* answers: *avirodhaśhchandanavat* (2.3.23) 'Sandalwood does not need to be applied everywhere. Just rub it onto the forehead, and it will cool the entire body. Similarly, the soul—although residing in the heart—permeates consciousness throughout the body.' Another example illustrating this principle is the lightbulb. The lightbulb is fixed in one place while its light illumines the entire room.

Continuing our inquiry into the nature of the 'self', let us ponder over the next question.

Size of the Soul

The atma does not have a physical form or physical boundaries. So, defining its dimensions can be a tricky matter. Philosophers of Bharat present three views regarding the size of the soul:

1. ***Vibhu***: Some believe the soul is infinite, or *vibhu*. They see it as inseparable from God, Who is limitless.
2. ***Madhyamākār***: Others believe the atma is medium-sized, or *madhyamākār*.
3. ***Aṇu:*** Yet others assert the soul is tiny, or *aṇu*.

Let us delve deeper into each of these viewpoints.

1. **Is the atma boundless in size?** If it were indeed infinite, then the notion of going to heaven or hell after death would become irrelevant. The soul would theoretically permeate the realms of earth, heaven, and hell, obviating any need for transitions between these domains. The Vedas, however, state:

   puṇyena puṇya lokaṁ nayati pāpena pāpam
   ubhābhyāmeva manuṣhyalolam

   (*Prashnopanishad* 3.7)

   'If you do pious deeds, after death you will go to the celestial abodes. If you engage in sinful activities, you will be sent to the lower planes of existence. While if you engage in both

Similarly, if we prioritize sleep as our main goal, then God could make us a polar bear after death, so we could hibernate for many months at a stretch.

We must, therefore, utilize our human form carefully and not fritter it away in fleeting pleasures of the senses.

Determine Your Highest Purpose

As humans, we can consciously decide our life's purpose and strive to attain it. Yet, most people never ponder about their ultimate goal. They meander purposelessly through life without a clear direction.

A traveller asked a bystander, 'Am I on the right path?'

The bystander responded, 'Where do you wish to go?'

The traveller replied, 'I do not know.'

'If you have no goal in mind' the bystander said, 'then it does not matter which path you take.'

Similarly, many people flounder aimlessly throughout life, from childhood to youth to old age, confused about their purpose. For a successful life, however, it is important to think deeply about one's ultimate goal.

What is it that we all are looking for? What is the underlying aspiration that drives us all?

The Search for Happiness

The Vedas say we all seek happiness in everything we do. We

may have different ideas regarding where we might find joy. One may feel that if only he could get a bigger car, he would be happy. Another thinks if she could get a nice house, she would become blissful. Someone else believes by becoming rich, he would be happy; while yet another feels if she could become a movie star, she would be joyous. Do note, everyone's common goal is happiness. And everything we do throughout the day is in search of happiness.

Where did this urge for happiness come from? Did someone explicitly teach us to seek bliss? Everything else in life had to be learnt. When we were small, we were taught, 'My child! You should always speak the truth.' 'Son, you should obey and respect your elders.' We were trained to read, write, and speak. However, we were never expressly taught, 'My child! You must always seek happiness. It should not happen that you start loving misery.' This instruction was never given to us. This implies we instinctively began seeking bliss without ever being taught to do so.

In fact, we expressed our desire for happiness the moment we were born. We did not say it in words since we could not speak. Instead, we did it by crying out with all our might. That is the first thing a newborn does. In the process of birth, it experiences pain, and it cries to reveal its nature. 'I have not come into this world for pain. I have come for bliss. Give me happiness!'

From that point onwards, all our actions are motivated by the pursuit of happiness. Hence, we can safely conclude that the goal of all living beings is happiness.

God is the Ocean of Divine Bliss

Why do we all want happiness? Only the Vedic scriptures alone answer this question satisfactorily and with a compelling explanation. They declare that we seek happiness because God is an Ocean of bliss.

ānando brahmeti vyajānāt (*Taittiriya Upanishad* 3.6)

ānandamayo'bhyāsāt (*Vedant Darshan* 1.1.12)

ānanda siñdhu madhya tava vāsā (*Vinay Patrika* 136.2)

Anand means bliss. The above verses state that God is an Ocean of unlimited bliss. We souls are His tiny parts. Hence, we are fragments of the Ocean of bliss. Shree Krishna told Arjun:

mamaivaṁśho jīvaloke jīvabhūtaḥ sanātanaḥ

(Bhagavad Gita 15.7)

'All the souls in the world are My eternal parts.' For example, a stone is a part of the mountain, a drop of water is a part of the ocean, and a ray of light is a part of the sun. Similarly, we souls are small fragments of God.

It is the nature of every part to be attracted towards its source. A lump of mud is a part of the earth and is drawn to it. If you throw a mud ball up, it will automatically fall down, pulled by Earth's gravity. Newton discovered this gravitational force when an apple fell on his head.

In the same way, the soul is naturally attracted towards its source, God. Since He is an Ocean of infinite bliss, we too, desire happiness in all we do. Not only that but we have been searching for it since endless lives. The problem, however, is that we have not found true joy until now. What is the reason for it?

The Mistake We Made

The reason we are bereft of true happiness is ignorance of the 'self'. We have forgotten we are divine souls and think of ourselves as the gross body. As a result, we search for material happiness and hope the soul will find satisfaction from it. But this is impossible as this example illustrates.

If you take a fish out of the water, you may massage it in scented oil and shove food down its throat, but this will never make it happy. The poor fish cannot speak, but if it could, it would say, 'I do not want all this. I will only be happy when you put me back in the water.'

Likewise, the soul is divine, and the happiness it seeks is also divine. But the happiness we are running after is the opposite. We are savouring ephemeral pleasures of the bodily senses. Despite our best efforts, the soul from within says, 'This is not my bliss; I am still unsatisfied. Give me divine bliss.'

Our soul wants divine bliss, which is of the nature of *sat*, *chit*, and *anand*. *Sat* means permanent, *chit* means ever-fresh, and *anand* means infinite bliss. Consider these individually:

1. **Our soul wants *sat* happiness**, or a permanent state of bliss. Worldly pleasures do not fulfil this yearning. They give us only a fleeting experience of enjoyment. For example:

   Suppose someone says, 'I had a great time yesterday. We went to the football game and had a lot of fun.'

   You ask him, 'What happened today?'

   He says, 'Today my car was out-of-order, so I stayed at home. The TV and internet were also down, and I got terribly bored.'

'This means the happiness of yesterday went away today?'

'Yes, it did.'

That kind of happiness, which comes and goes, cannot give contentment to the soul.

2. **Our soul is looking for *chit* happiness**, which will remain ever-fresh. However, the pleasure of material delights keeps reducing.

   For example, when two people get married, they have great expectations of bliss, and say things like, 'We have found the love of our life and will live happily ever after.' But in a few years, the joy from each other wears off and boredom sets in.

   Consider another example to drive home the point.

   Suppose you go to see a new Bollywood blockbuster movie. The first time you watch the movie, it gives you great happiness.

   Then your friend arrives from out-of-town and says, 'Hey, I heard the new movie released last week is really good. Let us go and see it.' You do accompany him, but watching the movie no longer gives you pleasure.

   Finally, your uncle comes from the nearby village and says, 'Son, I am here especially for the new movie about which I have heard so much. Come with me to watch it.'

   You respond, 'Uncle, give me some other punishment, but please do not make me see the same movie a third time.'

   We can see how the pleasure from material things keeps decreasing. Clearly, it does not satiate our desire for joy that will always remain fresh.

3. **Our soul wants *anand***, or bliss that is unlimited in extent. Everyone can attest to the fact that material pleasures do

not fulfil this condition.

When you graduated from college, you thought if you could get your own car, you would be happy. A few years later, you purchased your very own four-wheeler and were delighted.

But then you turned your attention to the sedans your seniors were driving. So, you thought to yourself, *I need to become a crorepati (possessing 10 million rupees), then I will surely be happy.*

Suppose some years down the line, you reach this milestone as well. Will it satisfy you? No, because by then you will be looking at the arabpatis (possessing one billion rupees) and hanker to become like them, *I have only one crore, while this person has one arab.*

Finite happiness can never satisfy the soul, which is seeking *anand*, or infinite bliss.

In conclusion, our soul will only be content when it attains divine bliss. Such bliss must possess the three attributes of *sat-chit-anand.* Since we have not found divine bliss, we keep searching for it, and endless lifetimes have gone by.

The *sat-chit-anand* bliss that we are seeking is a synonym for God. He is the Ocean of divine bliss. Hence, the ancient poet Valmiki said:

loke nah isa vidyeta yo na rāmamanubrataḥ

(*Valmiki Ramayan* 2.37.32)

'There is no soul in this world who is not a devotee of the Lord.' No one wants the reverse of bliss, which is misery, and hence, everyone knowingly or unknowingly desires God. It means that the goal of our life is God-realization.

Now listen to another argument proving that we are all searching for the Supreme.

Our Love for Godly Qualities

We all innately love godly virtues, such as truthfulness, non-violence, justice, kindness, forgiveness, and so on. Nobody in the world can love lies. You may question, 'How is that so? There are so many people in this world who are habitual liars. Not everyone is truthful.'

Definitely, there are untruthful people in this world. However, if you tell them a lie, they will not like it. They will ask, 'Why did you lie to me?'

'But you speak lies yourself.'

'Yes, I do, but I want everyone to speak truthfully to me.'

You might have come across a popular expression: 'Honesty amongst thieves.' If a gang member lies to the gang leader, he gets annoyed. This goes to show that even the head of a gang expects truthful behaviour from his gang members. This intrinsic love for honesty is because it is an attribute of God, and as His little parts, we are naturally drawn to it.

Once, a thief returned home after a burglary. He counted his bounty and went to sleep, satisfied that he had committed a successful theft. At night, his home was burglarized by another thief. When the first thief woke up, he exclaimed, 'Who did this? Does he not know who I am? If I find him, I will kill him.'

Now ask him, 'You are a thief yourself, so why are you angry?'

'If I steal from others, that is okay. But I do not want anyone to steal from me.'

Look at the irony. Though he is a thief himself, he is infuriated when others steal from him.

These examples illustrate that we all desire kind, fair, and honest behaviour from others, regardless of how unjust, unkind, or dishonest we may ourselves be. Why is this so? The reason is that these virtues are intrinsic to God. And as His fragmental parts, we inherently love them. This again goes to show that—knowingly or unknowingly—we all are searching for the Supreme.

Hence, we can conclude that the ultimate goal of life is God-realization. Only by attaining the Supreme will we experience the peace, happiness, and satisfaction our soul has been seeking since endless lifetimes.

The Glorious Destiny of the Atma

The soul derives its brilliance from God. Consider the analogy of a vast fire and a tiny spark. The fire has the power to consume an entire forest. In contrast, a spark seems insignificant, but it too harbours the potential to set the forest ablaze. Similarly, as parts of the Supreme Divine Personality, we hold immense potential for growth.

God Himself desires to share His magnificence with us. In the Vedas, He is referred to as Brahman. Jagadguru Shree Kripaluji Maharaj elucidated the meaning of this word:

kinds of activities, in your next life you will come back to the earth planet.'

This Vedic mantra dispels the hypothesis of the soul being infinite in size.

2. **Is the soul medium-sized?** Let us deconstruct this hypothesis. Assume a finite value 'X', to represent the soul. It means the soul cannot reside in any life form of size less than 'X', else it will spill outside it. However, there are innumerable life forms in the world—ranging from the tiniest microorganisms to colossal whales. If the soul has a fixed size 'X', how will it fit into the life forms smaller than 'X'? Hence, the idea that the soul is medium-sized reaches a logical contradiction.

   Jain scriptures postulate that the size of the soul is the same as that of the body it inhabits. This, however, raises a dilemma for the process of reincarnation. For instance, if a soul occupied an elephant's body in one life, how will it fit into the diminutive pigeon's body in the next? The incongruity of such a transition becomes readily apparent.

3. **The soul is infinitesimally small.** This is the only viable option that remains. The Upanishads state:

   eṣho 'ṇurātmā *(Mundakopanishad 3.1.9)*

   aṇupramāṇāt *(Kathopanishad 1.2.8)*

   These Vedic mantras reveal that the atma is miniscule in size.

Immortality of the Soul

For the soul, there is neither birth nor death. There was never a time when it did not exist, nor will there ever be a time when it will cease to be. What we term as 'death' is merely the soul changing bodies. The body is like a set of clothes for the atma. Every morning, you change your outfit and put on a fresh one. Similarly, when the body becomes unfit to reside in, the soul departs to receive a new body. The process of giving up the old body is looked upon as 'death' and taking on a new body is called 'birth'. The Bhagavad Gita states:

vāsaṁsi jīrṇāni yathā vihāya
navāni gṛihṇāti naro'parāṇi
tathā śharīrāṇi vihāya jīrṇā
nyanyāni saṁyāti navāni dehī (verse 2.22)

'As a man sheds worn-out garments and wears new ones, likewise, the soul casts off its worn-out body and enters into a new one upon death.'

In many cultures, the dead body is buried, and the person is assumed to be lying in the grave. However, the soul is not in the grave; it has left for its journey to the afterlife. The buried body will soon be eaten by vermin and turn into dust. In the Hindu tradition, the dead body is not buried, rather, it is cremated, and prayers are offered for the departed soul.

The Concept of Rebirth

What is the rationale for believing we had births before this one? Well, without accepting the idea of rebirth, the world becomes a very irrational place. How would you answer a person who is born blind when he asks, 'What did I do to be suffering like this?'

Clearly, it cannot be the result of present-life actions. It cannot also be the will of God, Who is supremely benevolent. Why would God want anyone to suffer? The only logical explanation for being born blind is negative karmas in previous lifetimes. Without accepting the existence of past lives, the above question has no plausible answer.

A rabbi, Harold Kushner, discussed this issue in his book, *Why Do Bad Things Happen to Good People?* He had a son who suffered from an atypical disease called progeria, which causes premature ageing. Afflicted by it, Kushner's son began ageing from childhood itself. At 14 years, he displayed the symptoms of an 80-year-old, and then passed away.

Kushner was terribly disturbed by this traumatic experience. He could not find any suitable answer as to why his son had endured such suffering. His son had done nothing so evil as an infant to be given such affliction, and Kushner did not believe in previous births.

The Vedic philosophy, however, offers a perfectly logical explanation for such a scenario. With the concept of multiple births, it posits that suffering could well be a consequence of past life sins. This also explains why one is born in a rich family and has no shortage of worldly luxuries, while another is born in a poor household where even obtaining food is a daily struggle. Someone receives a keen intellect to excel in life, while another is born dull and unable to study. The difference is the result of karmas from past incarnations.

Remembering Past Lives

On accepting the idea of rebirth, the question arises: why do we not remember our past lives? The answer is that death is very painful for the soul. It erases most memories of the life gone by. Furthermore, birth is an even more painful experience, which wipes out remaining recollections of the previous life.

The soul, nevertheless, does retain a faint remembrance in infancy. The *Nyaya Darshan* states:

jātasya harṣhabhayaśhoka sampratipatteḥ (3.1.18)

If you observe a little baby, you will find it occasionally becomes fearful without any obvious reason. Likewise, it becomes happy or begins to cry without a visible cause. The *Nyaya Darshan* explains that this is because it is recalling events of past lives and reliving those feelings. As the baby grows older, impressions of this life leave a strong imprint and eventually obscure the fainter impressions of past lives.

Nevertheless, this rule does have exceptions. There are accounts of people across the world who have vivid recollections of their previous life. Their statements about their past birth have been examined by scientists and confirmed as true. The famous example of Shanti Devi, who had died as Lugdi Devi in 1925 in Mathura and was reborn in Delhi in 1926, was one such case validated by a high-profile team.

Forgetfulness of the Self

Most people live in a state of forgetfulness of their real 'self'. Compare this to a simple worldly example.

If you ask car drivers to introduce themselves, and they respond, 'I am a Mercedes', 'I am a Ford', or 'I am a Toyota', you will think them to be grossly ignorant. You asked for their introduction, instead, they announced the brand of their vehicle.

Similarly, when asked, 'Who are you?', we respond with our name, 'I am Bimala', 'I am Kamala', and so forth.

'But that is your name. You could adopt a different name tomorrow, if you so decide, but you would still remain the same person. So, you are not a name. Now tell me, who are you?'

'I am an Indian.'

'That is your nationality. If you change your nationality to American, you will still remain the same person. I am asking about YOU, and not your country.'

'I am a postgraduate.'

'That is your educational qualification. Tomorrow you could become a PhD. You are not your degree. Who are you?'

'I am a human.'

'That is your species; it is the designation of your body. In your next life, you could become a celestial being. You have no information about your real self?'

In this way, people think of the body and its designations as the 'real self'. On the spiritual journey, we must train our intellect to see ourselves as the divine soul seated within the body.

What activities does the soul perform while seated within? Does it merely act as an observer, devoid of any administrative responsibilities? Let us now understand the functions of the soul vis-à-vis the body.

Administrative Duties of the Soul

The Vedas present the analogy of a chariot to help us grasp the soul's executive position:

ātmānam rathinam viddhi śharīram ratham eva tu
buddhim tu sārathim viddhi manaḥ pragraham eva cha
indriyāṇi hayān āhur viṣhayāṁs teṣhu gocharān
ātmendriya-mano-yuktam bhoktety āhur manīṣhiṇaḥ

(*Kathopanishad* 1.3.3–1.3.4)

Imagine a chariot with five horses pulling it. They have reins in their mouths. The reins are in the hands of a charioteer. A passenger is sitting at the back of the chariot. In this analogy:

- the chariot represents the body
- the horses symbolize the five senses
- the reins connecting to the horses' mouths represent the mind
- the charioteer embodies the intellect
- the passenger seated behind signifies the soul dwelling in the body

Ideally, the passenger should provide guidance to the charioteer, who, in turn, should use the reins to steer the horses in the right direction. However, in this case, the passenger, the soul, is asleep so, the chariot is veering directionless:

- The senses (horses) yearn to engage in various sensory experiences to see, taste, touch, feel, and smell various things.
- The mind (reins), instead of controlling the senses, supports their desires.
- The intellect (charioteer), rather than directing the mind (reins), succumbs to the impulses of the senses (horses).

– Seated on this chariot, the soul (passenger) has been roaming in the material world since eternity.

In this way, in the materially conditioned state, the soul has relinquished control of the chariot. Instead, it is a passive observer, vicariously experiencing the pleasures and pains of the mind and senses.

However, if the soul awakens and takes charge, it can inspire the intellect. The intellect then assumes its rightful role as the charioteer and governs the mind. And the mind, in turn, manages the senses. Consequently, the chariot embarks on its journey to eternal welfare.

Now that we have learnt our true nature, the next question that naturally arises is, 'What is the purpose of our life?' We will take this up in the next chapter.

2
The Goal of Life

Importance of the Human Birth

According to the Vedic scriptures, there are 8.4 million life forms, and the soul could be born in any of these species. Amongst them, the human form is special because it possesses the power of discernment, which is why it comes with a greater responsibility.

Compare this to the analogy of bank managers and cashiers. Bank managers sit in comfortable offices, while cashiers work at the counter. However, the managers have greater responsibilities as well. If they choose to do only as much as the cashiers, then the bank will take away their facilities and reassign them to counter duties.

Similarly, God has especially equipped humans with the faculty of knowledge. But He also expects us to utilize this ability to learn about the Absolute Truth. Instead, if we make eating delectable food as the primary goal of our life, it will be a misuse of the human form. As a result, in our next life, God could make us a pig, where we would be able to eat from morning to night.

brahma vṛihatvāt asa baṛā jāko ādi na anta
baṛā bṛinhaṇatvāt asa aurana kare ananta

(*Bhakti Shatak* verse 51)

This verse states that the word 'Brahman' has two meanings:

1) Brahman is He who is infinitely big. This is self-evident since God encompasses innumerable universes within His being.
2) Brahman is He who makes others big. This second facet reveals the Lord's aspiration for His fragments to reach perfection akin to His own.

God wants us to achieve the supreme perfection that He has planned for us. It is a fallacy to think, *I will forever remain flawed and incapable of change.*

Swami Vivekananda beautifully articulated the potential of the soul:

> These prophets were not unique; they were men as you or I... They had attained this super-consciousness, and you and I can get the same... The very fact that one man ever reached that state, proves that it is possible for every man to do so...every man must eventually, get to that state, and that is religion.[1]

While we revere the saints of the past—Soordas, Tulsidas, Mirabai, Tukaram, Guru Nanak, Kabir, and Narsi Mehta, to name a few—placing them on an altar is not the ultimate

---

[1]'Complete Works of Swami Vivekananda, Vol. I, Raja Yoga, Chapter 7: Dhyan and Samadhi', *Essential Books of Ramakrishna Order*, http://tinyurl.com/2vbp8cex. Accessed on 5 February 2024.

objective. Instead, we too must seek to become like them. **Unfoldment of the infinite glory of the soul is the essence of spiritual science.**

Having understood the higher purpose of life, it becomes imperative to draw on wisdom of the Vedic scriptures for embarking on the spiritual journey. For this, let us first understand what these sacred books are, and what they teach. This topic shall be explored in the ensuing chapter.

3

Vedas—The Eternal Knowledge of God

To gain knowledge in any subject, such as physics, chemistry, mathematics, we read textbooks. How can we learn the subject of spirituality? Are there any books we can refer to? These books should be written by someone whom we can trust, so we are assured they are free from mistakes. Only then will we be convinced that they are the correct guidebooks for fashioning our life's journey. Such works are the Vedas.

Importance of the Vedas

These sacred texts are not the works of any human; God Himself revealed them. That is why they are called *apaurușheya*, or 'having no human writer'. If the Vedas had been created by any human, one could have doubted the authenticity of their content. However, when the source is the Supreme Divine Personality, then all scepticism ceases.

Besides, who can know God better than God Himself? Hence,

what the Vedas say about the Supreme is the perfect reference source for spiritual knowledge. Since they were revealed by God, they are regarded as the most sacred amongst all the Hindu scriptures and are given the highest seat. These Vedas are the ultimate authority on Hinduism.

bhūtaṁ bhavyaṁ bhavishyaṁ cha sarvaṁ vedāt prasidhyati

(*Manu Smriti* 12.97)

'Any spiritual principle is only acceptable if it conforms to the Vedas.'

History of the Vedas

To be precise, the Vedas are not the name of any one book, rather they are the divine knowledge of God. They have existed ever since He has existed, which is eternity. Each time the Supreme Entity creates the world, He reveals the Vedas in the heart of the first-born Brahma. The Vedic knowledge is then passed down by word of mouth from Guru to disciple. Another name for the Vedas, therefore, is *Śhruti,* or knowledge conveyed by hearing.

About 5,000 years ago, Sage Ved Vyas, who was an Avatar of God, presented the same Vedic knowledge in writing. He also divided the Vedas, which were one body of knowledge, into four—*Rig Veda, Yajur Veda, Sama Veda,* and *Atharva Veda*. As a result, he came to be known as Ved Vyas, or 'one who divided the Vedas into four parts.'

Modern day scholars recognize the *Rig Veda* as the oldest scripture and most ancient poetry of humankind. However, the words 'oldest' and 'ancient' are not accurate descriptions of its antiquity. The Vedas are sanatan (eternal), just as God Himself is eternal.

Language of the Vedas

These sacred works are in Sanskrit, language of the celestial abodes. Modern linguists acknowledge that Sanskrit possesses the most systematic grammar in the world. Computer scientists declared Sanskrit to be the most computer-friendly language. Yet, its grammar is so sophisticated that learning and mastering it requires 12 years of study. Historians are amazed at how, 5,000 years ago, people could fluently speak a language with such complex grammatical rules.

Sanskrit is recognized as the mother of many of the languages of Bharat, such as Telugu, Kannada, Marathi, Oriya, Bengali, Gujarati, Punjabi, and Marwari. Likewise, Latin is the mother of many of the European languages, such as English, German, French, and Spanish. Interestingly, when we compare Latin with Sanskrit, it becomes obvious that Latin grammar is a diluted version of Sanskrit grammar. This fact has been acknowledged by many Western scholars, as stated below:

> India was the mother-land of our race, and Sanskrit the mother of Europe's languages; that she was the mother of our philosophy, mother, through Arabs, of much of our mathematics, mother, through Buddha, of the ideals embodied in Christianity, mother, through the village community, of self-goverment and democracy.

> Mother India is in many ways the mother of us all.[2]
>
> —Will Durant, American historian and philosopher, world-famous author of *The Story of Philosophy*

> The *Sanscrit* language, whatever be its antiquity, is of a wonderful structure; more perfect than the Greek, more copious than the Latin, and more exquisitely refined than either yet bearing to both of them a stronger affinity, both in the roots of verbs and in the forms of grammar, than could possibly have been produced by accident.[3]
>
> —Sir William Jones, English philologist, master of 13 languages and knower of 28 more

Having peeked briefly into their glory, let us continue our tour of the Vedic scriptures.

Sections of the Vedas

Each Veda contains four sections: *Saṁhitā*, *Brāhmaṇ*, *Āraṇyak*, and *Upaniṣhad*.

1. *Saṁhitā*: These contain mantras (hymns) addressed to various celestial gods and to the Supreme Lord.
2. *Brāhmaṇ*: They describe the rituals, such as the yajnas (fire sacrifices), in which these hymns are sung.

---

[2]Durant, Will, *The Case for India*, Strand Book Stall, Mumbai, 2007, p. 3.
[3]Jones, Sir William, 'The Third Anniversary Discourse delivered 2 Feb 1786, by the President, at the Asiatick Society of Bengal', *Electronic Library of Historiography*, http://tinyurl.com/4mwan5m6. Accessed on 5 February 2024.

3. *Āraṇyak*: These discuss the meanings of the rituals and lead to philosophic inquiry.
4. *Upaniṣhad*: They are the philosophical texts revealing knowledge of God.

Vedanga

These are supplementary to the Vedas and assist in understanding them. There are six *Vedāṅgas*:

1. *Śhikśhā*: It contains the rules of chanting the mantras.
2. *Kalp*: It has the rules for performing the rituals.
3. *Vyākaraṇ*: It contains the grammar of the Vedas.
4. *Nirukti:* It is the dictionary of the Vedas.
5. *Chhand:* It is the study of the scales, melodies, and meters in which the Vedic mantras are sung.
6. *Jyotiṣh:* These are astrological texts.

Other Vedic Scriptures

Although the Vedas are the ultimate source of spiritual knowledge in the Hindu tradition, they are not easy to comprehend. Therefore, to elaborate their purport, many more scriptures have been written. These sacred texts do not deviate from the authority of the Vedas, rather, they attempt to explain the meaning of the Vedic teachings.

The most important amongst these scriptures are the *Itihās* and the Puranas. Their authenticity is confirmed by the Upanishads, which term them as the fifth Veda:

itihāspurāṇaṁ pañchamaṁ vedānāṁ vedaṁ

(*Chhandogya Upanishad* 7.2)

'Know the *Itihãs* and Puranas to be the fifth Veda.' Reading them helps clarify the purport of the Vedas.

Compare this to the constitution of a country. It contains statutes describing complex laws of the land. Supplementary to the constitution are commentaries written by senior lawyers and judges. These commentaries clarify the meaning more simply than the constitution itself. Hence, many students read only the commentaries, without even delving into the constitution.

Similarly, the Puranas and *Itihãs* are like the commentaries that shed light on the purport of the Vedas.

Itihas

These are historical texts—the Ramayan and the Mahabharat. They chronicle the history of two important descensions of God.

The Ramayan, authored by Sage Valmiki, narrates the Leelas (divine Pastimes) of Bhagavan Ram. Amazingly, it was written before Shree Ram descended on the earth. Valmiki, the great poet-sage, was empowered with divine vision, by which he foresaw the pastimes Lord Ram would enact. Consequently, he penned them down in the 24,000 most exquisitely composed Sanskrit verses of the Ramayan. These verses also impart lessons on ideal behaviour in various social roles, such as son, wife, king, and married couple.

The Ramayan has also been narrated in many regional languages of Bharat, thereby increasing its popularity amongst the people. The most famous among these is the Hindi Ramayan, *Ramcharitmanas*, written by the learned devotee of Lord Ram, Saint Tulsidas.

The Mahabharat was written by Sage Ved Vyas. It contains 100,000 verses and is considered the longest poem in the world. The divine Leelas of Bhagavan Shree Krishna are the central theme of the Mahabharat. It is full of wisdom and guidance regarding duties in all stages of human life. It is also imbued with bhakti, or devotion to God.

The Bhagavad Gita is a portion of the Mahabharat. It is a dialogue between Shree Krishna and Arjun that transpired at the outset of the Mahabharat war. The Bhagavad Gita is the most popular Hindu scripture, since it contains the essence of all spiritual knowledge, so eloquently described by Bhagavan Krishna Himself. It has been translated into nearly every language of the world. Innumerable commentaries have been written on the Bhagavad Gita since it was spoken five millennia ago.

Puranas

There are 18 Puranas, written by Sage Ved Vyas. Together, they contain 400,000 verses. These describe the divine Pastimes of the various forms of God and His devotees. The Puranas are also replete with philosophic knowledge. They discuss the creation of the universe, its annihilation, and its regeneration. They also narrate the history of humankind and the genealogy of celestials, great kings, and holy sages.

The most important amongst them is the *Bhagavat Puran*, also called the Shreemad Bhagavatam. It was the final scripture written by Sage Ved Vyas. In it, he reveals the highest dharma of pure selfless love for God. The Bhagavatam is respected as the *Amalātmā Puran* that is devoid of the allurements of material rewards.

The Puranas and the *Itihās* are parts of the Smṛiti texts. *Smṛitis* are those scriptures that have not been directly manifested by God. Instead, they were revealed in the hearts of Sages, who then transcribed them into manuscripts. Since the Sages remembered this knowledge on the inspiration of God, these sacred tomes are called *Smṛiti.*

Shad-darshan

They are next in importance in the hierarchy of Vedic scriptures. Six sages wrote scriptures highlighting particular aspects of Hindu philosophy. These became known as the *Ṣhaḍ-darshan*, or six philosophical works. They are:

1. *Mimāṁsā Darshan*: Written by Maharishi Jaimini, it describes ritualistic duties and ceremonies.
2. *Vedānt Darshan*: Written by Maharishi Ved Vyas, it discusses the nature of the Absolute Truth.
3. *Nyāya Darshan*: Written by Maharishi Gautam, it develops a system of logic for understanding life and the Absolute Truth.
4. *Vaiśheṣhik Darshan*: Written by Maharishi Kanad, it analyses cosmology and creation from the perspective of its various elements.
5. *Yog Darshan*: Written by Maharishi Patanjali, it describes an eightfold path to union with God, beginning with physical postures.

6. *Saṅkhya Darshan*: Written by Maharishi Kapil, it describes the evolution of the universe from prakriti, the primordial form of the material energy.

The above tradition of scriptures—starting from the Vedas to the *Ṣhaḍ-darshan*—is collectively referred to as *Nigam Shastras.*

Agam Shastras

They are complementary to the *Nigam Shastras*. 'Agam' means 'handed down by tradition' and shastra means 'scripture'. *Āgam Shastras* are comprehensive manuals outlining the rituals of worship and religious practices. They also provide guidelines for constructing temples and proper conduct for engaging in deity worship.

Apart from the holy scriptures mentioned above, the Hindu tradition has hundreds of other sacred books as well. It is impossible to describe them all here. Let it suffice to say that the Vedic scriptures are a vast treasure-house of divine knowledge revealed by God and Saints for the eternal welfare of all.

Respect for All the Scriptures of the World

Hindus respect the scriptures of all religions. Yet, they bear in mind the strengths and uniqueness of their own Vedic scriptures. What is this specialty?

A teacher reveals knowledge as per the level of the students whom they are imparting the knowledge to. The professor may be a PhD, but if she is explaining to first grade students, she will only teach 2 + 2 = 4. This does not mean that the professor knows only that much. On the contrary, students can only comprehend to that level. Likewise, various great Saints who descended on the earth presented the Absolute Truth based on the situation, the need of the times, and the depth to which people could understand.

Many holy books of the world motivate their readers to worship the Supreme Lord out of fear of condemnation to hell. Again, the temptation is offered that if they have faith, they will go to heaven and enjoy celestial delights. However, the concept of selfless love for God is left untouched. This is because those sacred books were directed at readers whose soul had not yet reached the level of refinement required for understanding more profound spiritual topics. Hence, the higher truths of God-realization could not be revealed to them.

Arjun, listener of the Bhagavad Gita, was a highly evolved soul. If Shree Krishna had instructed him on elementary topics, such as abstaining from theft, Arjun would have felt offended, 'Why is He instructing me like that? Does He doubt that I will steal?' To such an advanced student as Arjun, the Bhagavad Gita was spoken, which goes into the finer nuances and intricate aspects of spiritual science.

Praise for the Scriptures of Bharat by Western Scholars

The Vedic scriptures have garnered praise by numerous Western scholars who read them. These philosophers and intellectuals had expressed their thoughts on the Vedic texts:

> I owed a magnificent day to the Bhagavad Gita. It was the first of books; it was as if an empire spoke to us, nothing small or unworthy, but large, serene, consistent, the voice of an old intelligence, which in another age and climate, had pondered and disposed of the same questions which exercise us.[4]
>
> —Ralph Waldo Emerson, American philosopher

Henry David Thoreau, a famous American essayist, philosopher, and poet, during the 19th century has said:

> In the morning, I bathe my intellect in the stupendous and cosmogonal philosophy of the Bhagavad Gita..., and in comparison with which our modern world and its literature seems puny and trivial.[5]
>
> Whenever I have read any part of the Vedas, I have felt that some unearthly and unknown light illuminated me. In the great teaching of the Vedas, there is no touch of sectarianism. It is of all ages, climes and nationalities and is the royal road for the attainment of the Great Knowledge. When I am at it, I feel that I am under the spangled heavens of a summer night.[6]

---

[4]'The Influence of Bhagavad Gita', *Wikipedia*, http://tinyurl.com/47r6mbnz. Accessed on 5 February 2024.

[5]Thoreau, Henry David, *Walden on Life in the Woods*, Ticknor and Fields, Boston, USA, 1854, p. 318.

[6]Pandit, Bansi, *The Hindu Mind: Fundamentals of Hindu Religion and Philosophy for All Ages*, Second Edition, B&V Enterprises, USA, 1996, p. 343.

> When we read with attention the poetic and philosophical monuments of the East, above all, those of India,...we discover there many a truth, and truths so profound,...that we are constrained to bend the knee before the philosophy of the East and to see in this cradle of the human race the native land of the highest philosophy.[7]
>
> —Victor Cousin, French philosopher

Arthur Schopenhauer, a German philosopher of the 18th century, had such a high regard for the Indian scriptures that he said:

> If the reader has also received the benefit of the Vedas, the access to which by means of the Upanishads is in my eyes the greatest privilege which this still young century may claim before all previous centuries...[8]
>
> In the whole world there is no study,...so beneficial and as elevating as that of the Upanishads. It has been the solace of my life, it will be the solace of my death![9]

---

[7]Woodroffe, Sir John, *Is India Civilized: Essays on Indian Culture*, Ganesh & Co., Madras, 1918, p. 111.

[8]Müller, F. Max, (ed.), *The Sacred Books of the East, Vol. 1*, The Clarendon Press, Oxford, 1900, p. lix.

[9]Ibid, p. lxi.

> If these words of Schopenhauer required any endorsement I should willingly give it as the result of my own experience during a long life devoted to study of many philosophies and many religions.[10]
>
> —Professor Max Müller, German orientalist

> ...this 'focus of Indian religion [The Bhagavad Gita]' is also one of the clearest and most comprehensive summaries of the Perennial Philosophy ever to have been made. Hence its enduring value, not only for Indians, but for all mankind.[11]
>
> —Aldous Huxley, English writer

The gamut of Vedic scriptures is like a general department store that offers a multitude of wares. You must select the goods you need from its crowded shelves. Likewise, the Vedas contain a wide spectrum of instructions for all classes, starting from the most fundamental, all the way up to the most advanced. We must assess what class we are in and follow the teachings befitting our level. Hence, it is recommended we learn Vedic scriptures under the guidance of a Guru, or Spiritual Teacher. Let us discuss the topic of Guru next.

---

[10]Woodroffe, Sir John, *Is India Civilized: Essays on Indian Culture*, Ganesh & Co., Madras, 1918, p. 112.

[11]Prabhavananda, Swami, and Christopher Isherwood (trans), 'Introduction by Aldous Huxley', *The Song of God: Bhagavad Gita*, New American Library, 1958, p. 13.

4

The Spiritual Master

The Disease of Ignorance

In the material realm, we suffer from an affliction called ajnana, or nescience, which prevents us from achieving our goals. We all want happiness but get misery. We want peace but experience conflict. We want to succeed but repeatedly experience failure.

We all know that anger, greed, hatred, envy, and pride are undesirable, which is why we wish to get rid of them. But we do not know how; if we did, we too could become like the Buddha.

A quarrelsome person came to the Buddha and began heaping abuses upon Him. The Buddha serenely kept listening to the offender. After an hour, the person got exhausted and became quiet. The Buddha told His disciples, 'He is tired. Give him something to eat and drink, so that he may begin again.'

That person was astonished. He said, 'Sir, are You made of wood or stone? Do You have no feelings? I abused You so maliciously, but You did not even complain!'

The Buddha said, 'My dear fellow! If you give someone a gift and that person does not take it, with whom does the gift remain?'

'With the person who gave it.'

'Similarly, I did not accept all that you gave so, it is still with you.'

This incident reveals that the Buddha had eliminated ignorance and was situated in knowledge. We, on the other hand, are far from such a state—we become infuriated if even one unpleasant sentence is spoken to us. Thus, our anger, greed, and envy are evidence of the nescience within us. The *Adhyātma Ramayan* states:

ajñānamevāsya hi mūla kāraṇaṁ. (*Uttar Kand* 5.9)

'Ignorance is the root cause of all our problems.'

We must, therefore, strive to remove ajnana and make our life successful.

Understand the Scriptures from a Guru

To acquire material knowledge, we read textbooks and go to teachers, who explain their meaning to us. Spiritual knowledge must also be acquired in a similar manner—through books and teachers.

The Vedic scriptures are not amenable to self-study, for they are incredibly intricate and complex. The Mahabharat states:

śhrutirvibhinnā smṛitayo vibhinnāḥ
naiko muniryasya vachaḥ pramāṇam

(*Varna Parva* 313.117)

'The scriptures are so many—*śhrutis* and *smṛitis*—each expounding on different principles. Even great scholars become get baffled on reading them.' Likewise, the Ramayan states:

śhruti purāna bahu kaheu upāī,
chhūṭa na ạdhika adhika arujhāī

(*Uttar Kand* 7.116(B)-3)

'The *śhrutis* and *smṛitis* teach many techniques. Merely reading them does not provide clarity, rather it only increases the confusion.'

Hence, all these holy books advice that they must be studied under the tutelage of a Guru. The *Chhandogya Upanishad* states:

āchāryavān puruṣho veda (6.14.2)

'Only through a Guru can you understand the Vedas.'

Having understood the need for a Guru, the question arises, 'Who is a true guru?'

Qualifications of a Guru

The word 'guru' has been adopted in the English language to signify 'expert in the field'. Nowadays, it is common to call an expert by terms such as 'management guru', 'economics guru', and so on. Here we are discussing the Guru of spiritual wisdom. Whom can we call a true guru?

The *Atharva Veda* informs us of the qualities of a Guru. It states:

tadvijñānārthaṁ sagurumevābhigachchhet
samitpāniḥ śhrotriyaṁ brahmaniṣhṭham

(*Mundak Upanishad* 1.2.12)

'To realize the Absolute Truth, approach with faith a Guru who is both *śhrotriya* and *brahma niṣhṭha*.'

In this mantra, two qualifications for the Guru are mentioned:

1. The Guru must be *śhrotriya*, or knower of the scriptures. The Guru must be proficient in scriptural knowledge and must have the ability to impart it to us effectively.
2. The Guru must be *brahma niṣṭha*, or situated in God-consciousness. The simple logic is that only one who is God-realized can help others reach that state. This is common sense. We can give to others only what we ourselves possess. Blind people cannot show others the path. Illiterate people cannot teach how to read. Ignorant people cannot give others knowledge.

Accordingly, the Guru must possess both attributes: 1) be theoretically learned, and 2) practically realized. Shree Krishna refers to such a Saint as *tattva darśhi* (Seer of the Truth). He conveys to Arjun:

tadviddhi praṇipātena paripraśhnena sevayā
upadekśhyanti te gyānaṁ gyāninas tattva darśhinaḥ

(Bhagavad Gita 4.34)

'To get knowledge of God, approach a Guru. Surrender unto him, serve him with faith, and inquire submissively from him. He will impart divine knowledge unto you because he has seen the Truth.'

I was blessed to personally learn the Vedic scriptures at the lotus feet of such a *śhrotriya brahma niṣhṭha* Saint, Jagadguru Kripaluji Maharaj, who was also the fifth original Jagadguru in Bharat's history.

Veracity of the Guru's Teachings

In contemporary times, whether by fortune or misfortune, we find ourselves presented with access to numerous gurus. They offer a plethora of diverse ideologies and methods. The challenge arises in discerning which guru's interpretation holds true, and which is prejudiced. Is there a way to ascertain whether a Guru imparts the Absolute Truth rather than mere personal opinion? Fortunately, a means of validation does exist.

The authenticity of the Guru's teachings can be validated in two ways:

It should concur with the sacred texts. Any deviation from these can raise doubt about the teachings being mere mental concoction. Even the slightest discrepancy in knowledge can erode its reliability.

It should concur with the teachings of past Gurus. The Absolute Truth is not a novel discovery but a timeless reality. Throughout Bharat's history, numerous enlightened beings, such as Soordas, Tulsidas, Meerabai, Kabirdas, Narsi Mehta, Shankaracharya, Madhvacharya, Ramanujacharya, Nimbarkacharya, Chaitanya Mahaprabhu, and Vallabhacharya have illuminated the path to it. Our Guru's teachings should also align with the foundational principles of these revered predecessors.

This validation process relies on the triad of Guru (our Spiritual Master), Sadhu (the numerous past Gurus throughout history), and Shastras (the Vedic scriptures). When these three—Guru, Sadhu, and Shastras—concur to affirm the same principle, we can confidently conclude that our Guru has imparted the correct knowledge of the Absolute Truth.

Follow the Instructions of the Guru

Once we find a God-realized guru, we must then diligently adhere to his instructions. This is just as when we are sick, we go to a doctor. We explain our symptoms to the doctor. Beyond that, we do not use our intellect; we trust his expertise. The doctor diagnoses our problem and tells us the remedy: 'Take this medicine, two tablespoons, three times a day, for one month, and you will be cured'. We follow the doctor's instructions and get well.

Now suppose, we used our intellect, *The doctor has told me to take a little medicine every day for one month. Let me take it all today, so that I will get cured in one day itself.* If we were to do this, the doctor would not be able to treat us. Similarly, the Guru can only cure us from the disease of ignorance if we follow his instructions.

But first, we must learn the secrets of the scriptures from the Guru, and then, we must act in accordance with the instructions.

Have Staunch Faith in the True Guru

Faith in the Guru's divinity is necessary for accepting their divine teachings. We are often unable to grasp the Guru's profound guidance due to our limited intellectual capacity. This is where faith is key. It enables us to wholeheartedly embrace even the Guru's most esoteric teachings and earnestly commit ourselves to sadhana (spiritual practice). As we progress on the path, the wisdom of these teachings gradually become evident.

True gurus are devoid of personal desires. They have merged their will with the will of the Supreme Lord. They are also free from pride and self-seeking propensity. Such Gurus do nothing of their own accord. Their actions are guided and inspired by God from within. Hence, these Gurus become instruments through whom the Lord performs His divine works of uplifting souls. Such Gurus become representatives of the Supreme in this world. This is why it is commonly said:

guruḥ brahma guruḥ viṣhṇuḥ guruḥ devo maheśhvaraḥ
guruḥ sākśhāt parabrahma tasmai śhrī gurave namaḥ

'Respect your Guru as you would respect God. Look upon him as the veritable form of Brahma, Vishnu, and Shankar.' The *Shwetashvatar Upanishad* states:

yasya deve parā bhaktiḥ yathā deve tathā gurau
tasyaite kathitā hyarthāḥ prakāśhante mahātmanaḥ

(mantra 6.23)

'For those who engage in devotion with unflinching faith in Guru and God, the import of all the Vedic scriptures is revealed in their hearts.' Such is the power of faith in the true Guru.

A story from the Mahabharat of Aruni, disciple of Rishi Ayoda-Dhaumya, illustrates the significance of faith.

Aruni was a prominent student of Rishi Ayoda-Dhaumya. He hailed from Panchala. Once, Dhaumya learned of a breach in his field's watercourse that could flood and destroy his crops. He summoned Aruni and asked him to fix it. Aruni respectfully agreed and went to the field.

Upon reaching the spot, he encountered a significant breach that could not be repaired by any means at his disposal. He devised a unique solution. Without hesitation, he lay down against the gap, using his body as a barrier, throughout the night and into the next morning.

Realizing Aruni had not returned, Dhaumya, along with the other disciples, arrived at the field to locate him. The Sage called out for his disciple. Upon hearing his Guru's voice, Aruni replied from a distance, 'Acharya, I am safeguarding the watercourse with my body. If I get up, the water will flood in and ruin the field. So, I am sorry, I cannot get up.'

Moved by Aruni's wholehearted devotion, Ayoda-Dhaumya approached the spot and said, 'Oh Aruni, through this act of unparalleled devotion, you have truly won your Guru's heart. You may rise now. As a symbol of your rising and reopening the watercourse, you shall henceforth be known as Uddalaka. Furthermore, because you followed my words without a single question, you shall attain immense fortune and respect in this world. All the Vedas and Dharmashastras will shine within you!'

The story exemplifies the profound effect of genuine faith. From the Guru, we must now learn the Absolute Truth and the path to God-realization.

5

The Nature of God

In the last four chapters, we established the foundations for the spiritual quest. We learnt we are the atma, or divine souls, and life's ultimate goal is God-realization. The attainment of this supreme goal requires knowledge of the Vedic scriptures, which must be learned under a true guru.

Let us now clarify some basic concepts about God. Detailed knowledge will come later. Is there a God? If so, who is He? And should we believe in Him merely on faith, or is there any proof of His existence? These are perennial questions that have been raised innumerable times in history. Even today, they arise in the minds of many people. We will delve into them, step by step.

Creator of the World

We live in an astonishing universe embracing the smallest atoms to the largest galaxies. How did creation come about? Some scientists propose the 'Big Bang' theory to explain it. They claim there was a big mass of concentrated matter. It exploded and scattered debris everywhere. Eventually, as this matter cooled, the world came into existence.

The Big Bang theory was initially proposed by Spinoza, Lucipus, Democritus, and other philosophers. It has now become the prevailing viewpoint of the scientific community. However, questioning its logic, I like to relate a humorous anecdote.

Maxwell, one of the greatest scientists in history, was a firm believer in God. His fellow scientist, a close friend, did not believe there was a God. He would argue that the world was made by itself. One day, Maxwell created a model of the solar system and set it in motion in his study room.

His friend came to meet him and on seeing the model, exclaimed, 'This is remarkable! Who made it?'

'Nobody made it,' Maxwell replied. 'I was working on my table when I heard an explosion. On turning around, I saw this had been formed.'

'How preposterous!' his friend retorted. 'Can such an incredible thing appear merely by an explosion? Someone must have definitely built it.'

'My friend, you are not willing to believe that a little model of the solar system could be created by itself,' said Maxwell. 'And you want me to believe that the real universe, consisting of many such solar systems, came into existence without a Creator. If it is logical to believe that this model has a maker, it is equally sensible to affirm that the real world must have a Creator too.'

This is exactly how the *Taittiriya Upanishad* describes God:

yato vā imāni bhūtāni jāyante yena jātāni jīvanti
yatprayantyabhisaṁviśhanti (3.1)

'God is He, Who created this world; God is He, within Whom the entire world exists; God is He, into Whom the whole world will merge on annihilation.'

Let us reinforce this definition of God's existence with another anecdote.

A geography teacher taught her students that the world was created by itself. She then asked them to make a map of the world, as their homework, and bring it the next day.

One of the students disagreed with what the teacher had taught. He decided to play a prank on her. The following day, he scribbled lines on a sheet of paper and filled it with random colours. He discreetly placed his sheet in the pile of submissions from the other students.

The teacher entered the classroom and began evaluating the maps on her table. When she came to that scrap of paper, she was infuriated. 'Who did this?' she exclaimed. The entire class fell silent. 'Tell me who did it, or I shall punish you all,' she said.

The student who had made it stood up. 'Ma'am! In my opinion, no one made it,' he said.

'What do you mean?' inquired the teacher.

'Possibly, the paper flew and landed on your desk,' the student replied. 'The pencil flew and scribbled lines on it. The colours flew and got filled in the paper.'

'How is that feasible?' the teacher retorted. 'Obviously someone

must have made it. And I strongly suspect you are the one.'

'Ma'am! You are not willing to believe that a distorted map of the earth could be created by itself. Yet, you want us to believe that the real world, consisting of innumerable planets, was created on its own? Just as it is reasonable to assume the map has a maker, it is also logical to conclude the real world has a Creator.'

The *Vedant Darshan* defines God along these lines. Its first aphorism states:

'athāto brahma jīgyāsā (1.1.1)

'Now try to know God.' This leads to the question, who is this God that we should know?

The second aphorism of the *Vedant Darshan* explains who God is:

janmādasya yataḥ (1.1.2)

'God is He, Who has created this world.'

Many Names of the One God

The Hindus worship Bhagavan, Christians venerate Christ, Muslims worship Allah, Jews uphold Yahweh, Parsis worship *Ahura Mazda*, Jains honour *Alakh Niranjan*, Sikhs revere *Ik-Omkar*, and Buddhists pay homage to *Shunya*. Are all these different Gods?

Sometimes religious practitioners develop intense enmity towards each other based on the God they worship. The *Rig Veda* dispels such misgivings. It clearly states:

ekaṁ saṅtaṁ bahudhā kalpayanti (10.114.5)

'There is One Supreme Entity, Whom Saints have referred to in various ways.'

The Creator of the world is One, and all religions worship the same all-powerful God. Quarrels are due to a lack of understanding. It mirrors the parable of the blind people who went to see an elephant.

One blind person put his hand on the elephant's stomach and exclaimed, 'This creature is just like a wall.'

The second blind man caught the leg and stated, 'This is a tree.'

The third held its tail and said, 'No, it's a rope.'

The fourth touched the elephant's ear and said, 'It is like a fan.'

Sticking to their views which were mutually contradictory, they began fighting with each other. One man was watching these blind men quarrelling. He pacified them, 'Do not fight. None of you is wrong. Each of you is describing parts of the same elephant. All that you have said together depicts the complete elephant.'

Similarly, the Vedas, with the eyes of knowledge, tell us not to quarrel on the basis of religion. They advocate respect towards all religions, explaining that they worship the same all-powerful Creator, but address Him by different Names.

ekaṁ sadviprāḥ bahudhā vadanti (*Rig Veda* 1-164.46)

'The Absolute Truth is one, yet scholars worship Him in various Forms.'

Does God Have a Form?

This question has often sparked debate with some arguing He

cannot possess a form. They contend that Krishna, Ram, Shiv, and others cannot be God for They possess a discernible form, while God is only formless. However, such an understanding of the Supreme Entity is very limited.

The fact is that God is all-powerful. He created this world that is teeming with shapes and forms. If He can create these myriad forms, does He not have the ability to adopt a form for Himself? Of course, He does. If we accept that He is omnipotent, then we must also affirm His ability to take a form. At the same time, God is also formless. Otherwise, His Divine presence would not be everywhere.

We individual souls also have both aspects to our personality. The soul is formless, yet, it has donned a human body—not just once, but innumerable times in countless past lives. When we tiny souls have this ability, definitely the all-powerful God can also adopt a form. Hence, the *Brihadaranyak Upanishad* states that He is both formless and with a personal form:

dwe vāva brahmaṇo rūpe mūrtaṁ chaiva amūrtaṁ cha

(verse 2.3.1)

'God is all-pervading, but He also manifests in a personal form.'

Further, is God male or female? The *Shwetashvatar Upanishad* asserts that He is both:

tvaṁ strī tvaṁ pumānasi tvaṁ kumāra uta vā kumārī (4.3)

'You are a Woman, You are a Man; You are a Youth and a Maiden too. You even manifested as an old person, tottering with a staff.' Hence, Narayan and Lakshmi, Krishna and Radha, Ram and Sita, Shiv and Parvati—all represent different Forms of the Supreme.

Language has its limitations. In the absence of universally accepted phraseology, I commonly use the term 'He' to refer to God. However, from the Vedic perspective, God encompasses both 'He' and 'She'.

The attributes mentioned above provide a mere glimpse of the Lord's countless divine qualities, serving to deepen our understanding of His eminence.

Many Forms of God

In Hinduism, we have many Gods—Krishna, Ram, Shiv, Vishnu, Durga, and more. Are they all different Gods, or are some bigger than others? The answer is that these are not separate Gods. They are various forms of the same Supreme Divine Entity. The scriptures state: *ekam-eva-advitīya ṁ bramha* 'There is one God without a second.'

Compare this to the various exterior appearances of your personality. When you go to the office, you dress up formally. At the park, you are clothed casually. And at home, you are relaxed in pyjamas. Now, your family members do not become confused, perceiving you as three different individuals. They understand these are only three different appearances. Similarly, Krishna, Ram, Shiv, and Vishnu are not distinct and separate Gods; they all are various forms of the same one Supreme Divine Personality.

The difference between God and us is that we are not all-powerful; we cannot exist in three places at the same time. However, God is supremely powerful. He can simultaneously manifest in as many forms as He wishes. Therefore, Krishna,

Ram, Shiv, Vishnu, and others are all His manifestations. True devotees respect all these divine Forms of the Lord, while choosing one of Them as their *Iṣhṭa Dev* (chosen form of God for worship).

Hence, we should not consider any one Form of the Lord as superior or inferior. Ved Vyas, who was an Avatar of the Lord, states in the *Padma Puran*:

sarve pūrṇāḥ śhāśhvatāśhcha dehāstasya paramātmanaḥ

'All the Avatars of God are perfect and complete.' The Supreme Divine Personality is so complete that He can simultaneously be both small and big, near and far, with a personal form and formless. Let us understand how.

God Possesses Innumerable Contradictory Attributes

The Vedic scriptures present an all-encompassing insight of the Supreme. They state that He possesses contradictory attributes at the same time. The *Brahma Puran* informs us:

asthūlo naṇurūposā vaviśhvo viśhva eva cha
viruddha dharmarūpo sā vaiśhvaryāt puruṣhottamaḥ

'God has countless paradoxical contrary qualities to His personality.' Elaborating on these opposing qualities, the *Shwetashvatar Upanishad* states:

aṇoraṇīyān mahato mahīyān
ātmā guhāyāṁ nihito 'sya jantoḥ (3.20)

'He is subtler than the subtlest, yet bigger than the biggest. He is present in the tiniest atomic particle, and yet, all of Creation resides in Him.'

These qualities may seem paradoxical, but they are not surprising considering that the Supreme Entity is all-powerful. The Upanishads state that He transcends all attributes:

neti natyasthūlamananuḥ (*Chhandogya Upanishad*)

'No description can circumscribe the Infinite. He is neither "big" nor "small".' This mantra is the opposite of the previous one, yet both hold true, illustrating the omnipotent nature of God.

Celestial Gods

What about the celestial devatas, such as Indra, Varun, Kuber, Agni, and Vayu? What is their status in comparison to the Supreme Divine Personality?

These devatas live in swarg, or the celestial abodes, which are higher planes of living within this material world. It is important to understand that devatas are not God; they are souls like us. They occupy specific administrative roles in the functioning of the world.

Consider the central government of the country. It has a home minister, a finance minister, an industries minister, an agriculture minister, and so on. These are positions that people occupy for a limited tenure. At the conclusion of the term, the post-holders change as the new government takes over. These posts are then assigned to different people.

Similarly, in the governance of the world, there are posts such as Agni Dev (the god of fire), Vayu Dev (the god of the wind), Varun Dev (the god of the ocean), Indra Dev (the king of the celestial gods), and others. Souls with substantial pious merit from past lives occupy these seats for a certain period. When their term is completed, others come to occupy the same seats. Thus, the celestial posts are given temporarily to souls and then taken away. We cannot equate devatas to the Supreme Lord, Who is the Master of the universe.

Many people worship celestial gods with the aim of seeking material rewards. However, these devatas can neither grant liberation from material bondage nor God-realization. Even if they do bestow material benefits, it is only by the powers they have received from God. Hence, Shree Krishna repeatedly emphasizes in the Bhagavad Gita that people who worship the celestial gods are less intelligent. Real wisdom lies in worshipping the Supreme Lord. In order to do that let us progress further in our journey towards God-realization.

6

How to Know God

In the previous chapter, we clarified some basic misconceptions about the nature of God. We must now get a deeper understanding of the Supreme Divine Personality. Ultimately, we would like to develop love for Him and attain God-realization. How will all this happen?

Knowledge Leads to Love

The Vedas inform us that if we wish to attain God, we must first obtain knowledge about Him. When we know Him, we will develop faith in Him, and through faith, we will attain love. The Ramayan states:

jāne binu na hoi paratītī, binu paratītī hoi nahiñ prīti

(*Uttar Kand* 7.88.4)

'Knowledge leads to faith, and faith leads to love.' Understand this principle through a worldly example.

Let us say, you are celebrating your birthday party. Your friends are coming one-by-one and offering you birthday gifts. Someone comes and gives you a ragged cloth bundle. You curl your nose in distaste, thinking, 'What is this dirty package?'

The person says, 'Don't jump to conclusions. Take a look inside.'

You untie the knot and find a gold brick in the bag. On realizing the value of the gift, you immediately place it against your heart. 'Oh wow! This is a real present. With this, I can buy anything I want.'

When you did not know the value of the gift, you had no love for it. When you came to know its worth, you immediately developed love for it. How did it happen? Knowledge resulted in faith, and faith resulted in love.

Similarly, if we can become aware of the greatness of God, the immense powers He possesses, and the extraordinary things He does, we will naturally develop faith in Him. Then, through faith, we will develop loving devotion.

Divine Knowledge Makes Us Grateful

Consider another benefit of the relationship between knowledge and love.

One man had a car accident in the countryside. His vehicle hit a lamppost and got crushed. The man lost consciousness inside the car. A villager came to the rescue. He checked the man's pockets, found his home address, and informed his relatives about the accident.

The villager took the man in his bullock cart to the nearest hospital. On checking the patient, the doctor advised an immediate blood transfusion to save his life. Without hesitation, the villager agreed to donate his own blood, which matched.

Upon regaining consciousness, the man found his relatives in the hospital room. He was overjoyed to see them. However, on noticing the villager, he frowned in disdain and inquired, 'What is this rustic doing here?'

The man's relatives informed him, 'This is the man who saved your life. He brought you to the hospital, gave you his blood, and apprised us about your accident. Had it not been for him, you would not be alive today.'

The man felt deeply indebted, 'I am thankful to you with all my heart. There is no way I can repay my debt to you.'

Earlier, without any knowledge of the villager's services he had received, the man had expressed disdain towards him. Simply by learning of the villager's selfless deeds, his attitude transformed, and he developed deep gratitude. Similarly, if we do not know who God is, how He is related to us, and what He does for us, we will foster neither faith nor love for Him. However, when we get to know Him, we will naturally develop great devotion.

The next question, then, is how can we know the Supreme?

God is Beyond Our Senses, Mind, and Intellect

We possess three instruments of knowledge—senses, mind, and intellect. We use these instruments to gather information about things.

If I were to show you a watch, and ask, 'What is this?' you would immediately reply, 'It is a wristwatch.' How did you arrive at this conclusion? Your eyes perceived the object and sent the information to the mind. The mind in turn processed the data, to understand its shape, size, and colour. The processed information was then sent to the intellect, which analysed the data and determined the object was a wristwatch.

This is how our senses, mind, and intellect learn about anything. However, these instruments of knowledge are incapable of knowing God. They are made from maya, the material energy, while the Supreme Divine Personality is not material; He is above maya. The *Mundak Upanishad* reveals: *divyo hyamūrtaḥ puruṣaḥ* (2.1.2) 'He, the Divine, is unfettered by form.'

Hence, God is beyond the purview of our senses. A hilarious story illustrates this point.

An animal trainer was the major draw in the circus where he performed. During his shows, lions, tigers, bears, and other animals would be released from their cages into the arena where he stood. Then, with the help of his whip and a four-pronged shield, he would tame them.

His show attracted many visitors, until a musician came to him and said, 'This is no big deal. I can make these animals dance to the tune of my violin.' His claim outraged the animal trainer who challenged the musician to prove his claim.

The musician accepted the challenge and sat in the arena, playing on his violin. First, the bear was released from its cage, and to everyone's astonishment, it got charmed by the music and began dancing. Then, the tiger was released, and it behaved in the same manner.

Finally, the lion was freed from its cage. The musician continued stringing his violin, but the lion was unimpressed. It began roaring fiercely and eyeing the musician. As it drew closer, the musician threw away his violin and ran for safety.

He asked the animal trainer, 'I have always succeeded in encharming creatures with my talent. Why did it not work on the lion?'

The animal trainer responded smugly, 'I knew it would not work. The lion is deaf and cannot hear.'

When it comes to perceiving divine subjects, we are equally blind and deaf. Our eyes can only see material things. Our ears can only hear material sounds, our skin can only touch material objects, and our tongue can only taste material foods. On the other hand, God is divine, and hence, He cannot be known by our senses, mind, and intellect.

Does this mean we will never attain God? Definitely not! Innumerable Saints, such as Shankaracharya, Madhvacharya, Nimbarkacharya, Chaitanya Mahaprabhu, and Vallabhacharya have seen God, spoken to Him, known Him, and realized Him. But they also had material senses like ours, then how did they come to know God?

To find the answer to this riddle, we must once again turn to the Vedas. They are the ultimate authority for Brahma jnana, or knowledge of God.

Know God through His Grace

The *Yajur Veda* states that the Supreme can be known only by His mercy:

tasya no rāsva tasya no dhehi

'Without the grace of the lotus feet of God, nobody can know Him.'

When God bestows His grace, He will endow His divine power to our material senses, mind, and intellect. Equipped with His power, we will be able to see Him, know Him, and love Him. Those fortunate souls who received His grace became God-realized saints. We have not yet received this extra special grace, which is why we are still rotating in the 8.4 million species of life. The Ramayan beautifully states:

soi janai jehi dehu janai, janata tumahin tumhahin hoi jai

(*Ayodhya Kand* 2.126.2)

'Only those can know You, Oh Ram, upon whom You bestow Your divine grace. And such fortunate souls become godlike.'

When the Lord graces us, He will bestow His divine power upon us. He will add His divine eye to our material eyes, His divine mind to our material mind, and His divine intellect to our material intellect. When our senses, mind, and intellect become divine, endowed with His power, then we too will be able to know Him.

Jagadguru Kripaluji Maharaj explained this very nicely in the *Bhakti Shatak*:

samujh! samujh saun śhyām ko, samujh sakā nahin koy
samujh milai jab śhyām kī, samajh sakai bas soy

(verse 32)

'By their own effort, nobody can ever know Shree Krishna. When He Himself bestows His grace upon someone, then that fortunate soul attains knowledge of the Lord.'

If God-realization depends upon grace, then is there no need for self-effort? Can we sit passively and wait for the grace to descend upon us? Or do we need to do something to become benefactors of this special grace? This question will be addressed next.

7

The Importance of Self-Effort

In the previous chapter, we understood the need for God's grace to know Him. Does this mean there is no importance of self-effort? Should we then stop all our sadhana and simply wait for His grace?

Understand the answer through a humorous story.

A villager was transporting wheat bags to town on his bullock cart. On the way, the cart's wheels got stuck in the mud. The villager was an ardent devotee of Lord Hanuman. He took out the Hanuman Chalisa prayer book and began reciting it. When done, he folded his hands and prayed, 'Oh Hanumanji! Please come and free my cart from the mud.'

Seeing nothing happening, he started reciting the Hanuman Chalisa once more. On completing it, he again prayed in the same manner. Hanumanji was hearing the villager's pleas. He thought, This person is devoted, but his understanding of God's grace is incorrect. Let me teach him.

Hanumanji manifested before the villager and said, 'My dear fellow, if I start taking out people's carts in this manner, the whole world will become lazy. Instead, you put in your best effort. Stand with your feet in the mud, and push the cart with all your might while calling out to the bulls. Simultaneously, pray to Me for My grace. Then I will add My strength to yours, and you will be able to take the cart out. However, if you think you will not do anything and Hanumanji alone should get the work done, that will never be.'

The story illustrates the grace of God is necessary, but our effort is also required. The *Shwetashvatar Upanishad* says:

tapaḥ prabhavāddevaprasādāchcha (6.21)

'Our own effort and the grace of God are both essential for attaining the ultimate goal.'

We Have the Free Will to Act

Many people downplay the significance of personal effort, claiming, 'Nothing is within our control. God resides within us, guiding all our actions.' In the *Pandav Gita*, the wicked Duryodhan employed similar reasoning:

jānāmi dharmaṁ na cha me pravṛittiḥ
jānāmyadharmaṁ na cha me nivṛittiḥ
kenāpi devena hṛidisthitena
yathā niyuktosmi tathā karomi

Duryodhan said: 'I know what is right, and I also know what is wrong. But there is some devata sitting inside me. As he provokes me, that is how I behave.'

Many people often present such arguments. When questioned about their mistakes, they attribute them to the will of God.

Their explanation goes like this: 'It is God Who orchestrates all events, and we are but puppets in His hands.' They even provide scriptural verses in support of their standpoint.

umā dāru joṣhita kī nāīṅ, sabahi nachāvata rāma gosāīṅ

(Ramayan, *Kishkindha Kand* 4.10.4)

'Just as a puppeteer gets wooden dolls to dance, the Lord is making us dance to His tune.' Consequently, we are not responsible for our actions.

A common saying among people captures this sentiment: *binā bhagvān kī kṛipā ke ek pattā bhī nahīn hilatā* 'Without the will of God, not even a leaf moves.'

On hearing this, people become reassured, 'It means God is the Doer of all our actions, so we need not bother about improving them.' However, this is incorrect thinking. If God were indeed our Director, we would never have committed any mistakes. All of our actions would have been perfect since God can never make a blunder. The fact that we err repeatedly implies we are performing actions of our own free will.

Further, if God were our Doer, we would not receive karmic reactions. Why would we suffer for what God did through us? He would either bear the karma or forgive Himself. However, the Law of Karma states:

karama pradhāna visva kari rākhā
jo jasa karai so tasa phalu chākhā

(Ramayan, *Ayodhya Kand* 2.218.2)

'The world is under the wheel of karma. In accordance with our actions, we receive the results.' The existence of the Law of Karma suggests that we are the doers of our actions.

God is impartial and perfectly just. If He were responsible for our actions, He would either have made everyone perform good deeds and become Saints, or He would have made everyone perform wicked actions and become demons. But there is so much diversity in the world. One is a Saint, like Prahlad, while the other is a demon, like Hiranyakashipu. This variety implies we possess the freedom to choose and are responsible for what we do.

Finally, if God were the Inspirer of our actions, there would be no need for Him to speak the Bhagavad Gita or any other scripture. He would not have to explain the path to perfection. Only two sentences would be required: 'Oh souls, I am the Doer of everything. So, you need not understand proper and improper action.' Yet, even at the end of the Bhagavad Gita, Shree Krishna states:

iti te jñānam ākhyātaṁ guhyād guhyataraṁ mayā
vimṛiśhyaitad aśheṣheṇa yathechchhasi tathā kuru (18.63)

'O Arjun, I have given you divine knowledge. Now, ponder over it deeply, and then do as you wish.'

Likewise, Lord Ram delivered a discourse to the inhabitants of Ayodhya, in which He said:

sunahu karahu jo tuhmahi sohāī

(Ramayan, *Uttar Kand* 7.42.2)

'Hear Me out, and then do as you wish.'

Certain passages in the Vedic scriptures refer to God as the Doer. So, it becomes imperative to learn about their context to avoid any misunderstanding. For this, understand two key terms: *prayojak kartā* and *prayojya kartā*.

Prayojak kartā: This term refers to the one who bestows the power to perform works. God is the *prayojak kartā*, as He provides our senses, mind, and intellect with the capability to engage in actions.

Prayojya kartā: This term designates the one who employs the bestowed power to work. The individual soul is the *prayojya kartā*, as it harnesses this divine power for its actions.

A good analogy is of the electrical station that supplies electricity to your house. If it did not provide power, you would not be able to do any electrical work. However, once you have the power supply at your home, what you do with it is your own choice. You could heat or cool the house, as you wish.

Similarly, God bestows our eyes with the power to see. What we see is our own choice. We could go to the temple and have darshan of the deities, or we could waste our time by watching movies and shows. God merely gives us the faculty of sight. He does not decide how we choose to use it.

Therefore, let us not shift the blame for our actions to God. If we make a mistake, it is our responsibility to acknowledge it, learn from it, and strive to prevent its recurrence.

However, taking ownership of our inadequacies is not easy. To evade it, some people resort to blaming destiny.

Destiny vs Self-effort

Some do not blame God for their errors; they hold their destiny responsible for it. They say we all were born with our individual destiny which determines our wealth, education, fame, lifespan, and health. Whatever is written in our fate will happen, no matter what we do. And what is not written, we will never get it, no matter how hard we try. Hence, there is no point in putting effort to accomplish anything.

Such excuse-makers even provide quotations to support their views.

yaddhātrā nija bhāla paṭṭa likhitaṁ
stokaṁ mahaddvādhanaṁ
tatprāpnoti marusthalepi natarāṁ
merau tato nādhikam
taddhīro bhava vitta vatsu kṛpaṇāṁ
vṛittiṁ vṛithā mā kṛithāḥ
kūpe paśyapayo nidhāvapi
ghaṭo ghṛṇāti tulyaṁ jalam

'Whether you immerse a pot in a well or an ocean, it will fill with the same volume of water. Similarly, you will only get as much wealth as is written in the pot of your destiny. Living on the golden Sumeru Mountain will not help you get more, and residing in the desert will not make you get less. Thus, putting in effort is futile.'

The above view is called fatalism, which is the belief that we are bound by an unalterable destiny. It asserts that all events are predestined to occur, rendering human beings powerless to alter their fate. Thinking in this manner results in an attitude of compliance and passivity, stemming from the belief that people are entirely helpless in the face of destiny.

Before scrutinizing the validity of the fatalistic doctrine, let us understand what destiny is. The scriptures state:

pūrva janma kṛitaṁ karma taddaivamiti kathyate
(*Hitopadesh*)

'The actions we performed in our past lives created our destiny in the present.'

This means destiny is not an ethereal decree bestowed from the celestial realms. Nor is it a cryptic chart unveiled by astrologers. Instead, our destiny has been crafted through the actions undertaken by our own volition in previous births. This implies that in prior lifetimes, we exercised our free will to perform actions.

Now, let us employ the technique of *Reductio ad absurdum* to disprove the fatalistic argument. Assume, for the sake of argument, that everything indeed is predestined. In that case, our current life is governed entirely by destiny and there is no scope for individual agency. However, this proposition must hold true for our previous lifetimes as well. Consequently, it would imply that in our past lives, we were similarly bound by destiny.

This line of reasoning creates a perplexing question. If destiny was binding us in all past lives, then when did we perform independent actions that forged our destiny? And if no prior life allowed us the freedom to act by our own volition, then how could destiny have been formed? Conversely, if we exercised our free will in any past life, it follows that we can do so in our present life as well. Hence, the premise that all events are predetermined reaches a logical contradiction.

Thinking in a fatalistic manner will make us lazy. We will assume, 'Everything is predetermined, so whether I work hard or not does not matter.' Such debilitating thoughts will impede our inspiration to try our best. Hence, the Ramayan states:

daiva daiva ālasī pukārā (*Sundar Kand* 5.50.2)

'Only lazy people blame destiny for their substandard achievements.'

To prevent falling into the fatalistic trap, let us try and understand what destiny truly is. There are three kinds of karmas associated with all of us:

Sañchit Karma: All the actions that we performed in endless past lives are noted by God, Who maintains their account. These are called *sañchit* karmas.

Prārabdh Karma: At the time of birth, God takes a portion from these accumulated karmas and gives them in the present life. This becomes our destiny and is called *prārabdh* (fate).

Kriyamāṇ Karma: Although *prārabdh* is fixed at birth, we still retain the freedom to perform new karmas. The actions we do in the present by our own agency are called *kriyamāṇ* karma. These are in our own hands and not predetermined.

What we get in life is the result of both the *prārabdh* and the *kriyamāṇ* karmas. Compare it with playing a game of cards. The hand of cards that is dealt to you is fixed. However, how you play is up to you. If you are a good player, you can win with bad cards. Instead, if you play badly, you could lose even with good cards. Similarly, if we put in sincere effort, we can succeed despite bad prārabdh. However, if we are lazy, we will fail despite a favourable destiny.

So, destiny does exist and will be given to us automatically; we should not worry about it. Instead, we should put in our best efforts to shape a bright future.

The Grace of God Must be Earned

In conclusion, the concept of grace of God should not diminish the need for self-effort in our minds. God is causelessly merciful and is waiting to bestow His grace upon us. However, He can only do so when we go to Him with a proper vessel.

If you went to a milkman with a leaking vessel and asked for a litre of milk, the milkman would say, 'I am ready to give it to you, but you will not be able to retain it. Bring a proper vessel, and I will pour in it.'

Similarly, we too will have to prepare the vessel of our heart to receive the grace of God. How can we qualify for His grace? This is the next question we will address.

8

Surrender to God

Let us now inquire as to how we can qualify for God's grace. And what criteria have prevented us from receiving it so far.

Why Have We Not Yet Received Divine Grace?

We hear that God is causelessly merciful. Then, why has He not bestowed His mercy upon us? Endless lifetimes have passed rotating in this cycle of life and death. How long will this continue? A devotee complains:

api garta mukhe gataḥ śhiśhuḥ
pathipi nivāryate javāt
janakena patana bhavārṇave
na nivāryo bhavatā kathaṁ vibhoḥ

'My Lord! If an infant has fallen into a ditch and is wailing, any passerby who sees the infant is moved to pity. They lift up the child, quieten it, and try to locate its parents. If the parents are not traceable, they give the child to an orphanage or police station. But no one in the world is so hard-hearted as to throw the little baby back into the ditch.

'Are You even worse than worldly people, Oh Lord? I hear that You are my Eternal Father. You are completely aware of my miserable condition in the world. You have the ability to uplift me with a simple glance of Your grace. Then why am I bereft of Your grace? Not once in innumerable lifetimes did You choose to make me Your own. On the other hand, You bestowed Your divine mercy on so many Saints in history.'

God responds to the accusation: 'Oh soul! You are urging Me to grace you on the grounds that I am your Father. When you visit the temple, you say: *tvameva mātā cha pitā tvameva* "Oh Lord, You are my Mother and Father." But I ask you, "Do you really believe I am your Father? You simply utter empty words in which you have no faith."'

God concludes by saying, 'I will bestow My grace the day you truly accept Me as your Father. Innumerable Saints did so in the past and attained eternal bliss. You too can do the same.'

God is just and unbiased. He governs the world as per His eternal laws. If He were to arbitrarily grace people, the world would lose their faith in Him. Consider the following example.

A father had two sons. He instructed both to go and work hard in his cornfields. The first son obeyed his father's instructions and toiled all day long. Upon his return, his father said, 'Well done my son! Here are a thousand rupees. Go and enjoy yourself.'

On the other hand, the second son did not go to the fields. He stayed back home lounging on his bed, glued to his smartphone.

He also drank alcohol and abused his father in a drunken state. Surprisingly, at the end of the day, the father rewarded the second son in the same manner, saying, 'Never mind! After all, you are also my son. Here, take a thousand rupees and have a good time.'

The consequence was that the first son lost his motivation to serve his father. He thought, 'If this is my dad's reward policy, then there is no point in exerting myself. Father will give the thousand rupees regardless.'

Likewise, God says if He were to confer His grace whimsically, the Saints would complain: 'My Lord, we endeavoured for many births and then became benefactors of Your grace. If this person, who did not obey Your instructions, has also received it, then our striving so hard to conform to Your laws was meaningless.'

Hence, God affirms, 'I do not break My rules. I have My laws in accordance with which I administer the world. If you wish to receive My divine grace, you will need to fulfil My condition for it.'

What, then, is the condition for receiving grace?

The Principle of Sharanagati

God's eternal law is very simple: Those who are *śharaṇāgat* (surrendered to God) receive His grace. All the scriptures, from the Vedas to the Ramayan, emphasize the principle of śharaṇāgati. Let us take a look.

The *Shwetashvatar Upanishad* of the *Krishna Yajur Veda* states:

yo brahmāṇaṁ vidadhāti pūrvaṁ
yo vai vedānśh cha prahiṇoti tasmai
taṁ ha devam ātma-buddhi-prakāśhaṁ
mumukṣhur vai śharaṇam ahaṁ prapadye (6.18)

'We take shelter of that Supreme Being who created Brahma and others. By His grace the soul and intellect get illumined.' The Shreemad Bhagavatam states:

mām ekam eva śharaṇam ātmānaṁ sarva-dehinām
yāhi sarvātma-bhāvena mayā syā hy akuto-bhayaḥ
(verse 11.12.15)

'O Uddhav! Giving up all forms of mundane social and religious conventions, simply surrender unto Me, the Supreme Soul of all souls. Only then can you cross over this material ocean and become fearless.' The Bhagavad Gita states this law:

tameva śharaṇaṁ gaccga sarva bhāvena bhārata
tatprasādāt paraṁ śhāntiṁ sthānaṁ prāpsyasi śhāśhvatam
(verse 18.62)

Shree Krishna says in this verse, 'Arjun, surrender yourself to God. Then, by His grace, you will attain perfect peace and the divine Abode.' The Ramayan also says:

sanamukha hoi jīva mohi jabahīṅ,
janma koṭi agha nāsahiṅ tabahīṅ (*Sundar Kand* 5.43.1)

'The moment a soul surrenders to God, its account of sinful deeds from endless past lifetimes is destroyed by His grace.'

Since all the scriptures recommend the act of surrender to the Supreme, let us delve into it more deeply.

The Nature of Sharanagati

Surrender has been defined in the *Hari Bhakti Vilās*, *Bhakti Rasāmṛita Sindhu*, the *Vāyu Puran*, and the *Ahirbudhni Saṁhitā* in the following manner:

ānukūlyasya saṅkalpaḥ, pratikulyasya varjanam,
rakṣhiṣhyatīti viśvāso goptṛitve varaṇaṁ tathā
ātma nikśhepa kārpaṇye ṣhaḍvidhā śharaṇāgatiḥ

(*Hari Bhakti Vilās* 11.676)

This verse explains the six aspects of surrender to God:

1. **To desire only in accordance with the desire of God**. By nature, we are His servants, and the duty of a servant is to fulfil the desire of the master. So, as surrendered devotees of God, we must make our will conform to the will of God.

   This can be compared to a dry leaf that is surrendered to the wind. It does not complain whether the wind lifts it up, carries it forward or backward, or drops it to the ground. Similarly, we too must learn to be happy in the happiness of God.

2. **Not to desire against the desire of God**. Whatever we get in life is a result of our past and present karmas. However, the fruits of these karmas do not come by themselves. God notes them and gives the results at the appropriate time. Since the results are dispensed by God Himself, we must learn to serenely accept them.

   Usually, when people get wealth, fame, pleasure, or luxuries in the world, they forget to thank God. But when negative circumstances come, they blame Him for it, 'Why did God do this to me?'

Surrender means to not complain about whatever the Lord wills for us, as depicted in this poignant story.

During Bhagavan Ram's journey through the forest of Dandakaranya, He reached Pampasar Lake and was extremely thirsty. He placed His bow down and stooped to take a drink of water from the lake. However, unbeknownst to Him, He had inadvertently rested His bow on a nearby frog.

After quenching His thirst, Lord Ram noticed the severely injured frog, its body marked by the weight of His bow. Moved by compassion, He said, 'My dear frog, what is this? You have endured such great suffering, yet you did not complain. I have granted you a voice. You could have cried out in pain, but you remained silent.'

The frog replied, 'My Lord, whenever I faced difficult circumstances in the past, I would cry out to my Supreme Master and Protector, Shree Ram. Today, Ram Himself has placed me in this predicament. Whom shall I cry out to now?'

The frog then added, 'I am not complaining. I accepted this as Your divine will. I prayed for strength to endure the pain.'

This story beautifully portrays that we must refrain from desiring outcomes contrary to God's will. **We must exert our best efforts and having done so, accept the outcomes as God's plan**. Complaining erodes surrender. True surrender means always saying, 'Yes, God'.

3. **To have firm faith that God is protecting us**. As our spiritual Father, He is taking care of all living beings in Creation. There are trillions of ants on the planet earth, and all of them need to eat regularly. Do you ever find that a few million ants in your garden died of starvation? God ensures

they all are provided for. On the other hand, elephants eat mounds of food every day. The Lord provides for them too.

Even a worldly father cares and provides for his children. Why then should we doubt whether our eternal Father, God, will take care of us or not? To have firm faith in His protection is the third aspect of surrender. Take inspiration from the little girl in this story.

A businessman rushed to catch his flight, barely making it to the boarding gate before it closed. He found himself seated next to a young girl. It struck him as unusual that she was traveling alone, but he refrained from commenting.

About an hour into the flight, the plane encountered sudden turbulence, leaving many passengers anxious. The businessman was tense too, gripping his seat and exclaiming 'Oh my God!' with each jolt.

In contrast, the little girl was remarkably composed. The man marvelled at her calmness and asked how she managed to remain tranquil while the adults were terrified. She looked into his eyes and replied, 'My father is the pilot, and he is taking me home.'

Likewise, God is our Father. We must make Him the Pilot of our life and repose our faith in His unwavering protection. His plans for us are always for our highest good and welfare. As they say, 'God's plan for us is always better than our plan for ourselves.' With this firm belief and inner conviction, we will become fearless in the midst of tribulations.

4. **To keep an attitude of gratitude towards God**. We have received so many priceless gifts from the Lord. The earth

we walk upon, the sunlight with which we see, the air we breathe, and the water we drink are all bestowed by Him. In fact, it is because of Him that we exist. He brought us to life and conferred immortality to our soul. We do not pay Him any tax in return. The least we can do is acknowledge these graces and feel indebted for them. This is the attitude of gratitude.

The reverse is the sentiment of ungratefulness. For example, a father tirelessly provides for his child, making immense sacrifices. The child is told, 'Be grateful to your father. He literally cut his stomach to feed you.'

But the child responds, 'Why should I be grateful to Papa? His father took care of him, and he is taking care of me. He is just doing his duty.' This is ingratitude towards the worldly father.

Cultivating gratitude towards our eternal Father for all He has given is the fourth aspect of surrender.

5. **To see all we possess as belonging to God**. The world existed before we were born and will continue to exist after we die. God is its Creator, and hence, He is the only true Owner of everything. Our claim to proprietorship is unjustified as the following example illustrates.

   Let us say that someone enters your home in your absence. He wears your clothes, eats out of your refrigerator, and sleeps on your bed. On returning, you ask indignantly, 'What have you been doing in my house?'

   He says, 'I have not damaged anything. I have merely used everything properly. Why are you getting annoyed?'

You reply, 'You may not have destroyed anything, but it all belongs to me. If you use it without my permission, you are a thief.'

Similarly, this world and everything in it, belongs to God. When we think something belongs to us, we lose sight of the spiritual principle that God is the true Proprietor of everything.

Rabindranath Tagore was a poet par excellence. The Nobel Prize he received for his anthology, *Gitanjali*, was just a little accolade for his immense ability. And yet out of his humbleness, he said, 'My Lord, everything that is good in my poetry is Yours. It has come from You. Everything that is bad is mine. It is because of my lack of surrender and my lack of complete connection with You that these blemishes are still there.'

To remember God's proprietorship—and give up our sense of ownership—is the fifth aspect of surrender.

6. **To renounce the pride of having surrendered.** If we become proud for our good deeds, it tarnishes our heart and undoes the good. That is why we must keep an attitude of humility, thinking, 'If I did something worthwhile, it was only because God inspired my intellect in the right direction. Left to myself, I would have never done it.' Keeping such an attitude of humility is the sixth aspect of surrender.

If we can fulfil these six points of surrender, we will meet God's condition. He will then bestow His grace upon us. The Bhagavad Gita states:

sarva-dharmān parityajya mām ekaṁ śharaṇaṁ vraja
ahaṁ tvāṁ sarva-pāpebhyo mokṣhayiṣhyāmi mā śhuchaḥ

(verse 18.66)

'Abandon all varieties of dharmas and simply surrender unto Me alone. I shall liberate you from all sinful reactions; do not fear.'

In this context, it is imperative to understand that the surrender must not be a mere external act.

Surrender Must Be of the Mind

Often, people engage in external rituals without devotional sentiments. They travel physically to sacred places, while their mind remains entangled in worldly matters. They cleanse their bodies in the waters of holy rivers, while overlooking their impure thoughts. They offer clarified butter in sacrificial fires but fail to offer the oblation of their ego to God. In the poojas, they adorn the deities but neglect to decorate their inner emotions.

However, the sacred Vedic texts emphasize that **spirituality is an inner journey. It is the unfolding of the divinity within us, requiring purification of the mind.** External rituals when done alongside with bhakti bhav can be very purifying. However, if not accompanied by the cultivation of noble sentiments, rituals get reduced to a physical drill that serves very little purpose. Hence, the *Panchadashi* states:

mana eva manuṣhyāṇām kāraṇam bandha mokṣhayoḥ

'Both bondage and liberation depend upon the state of our mind.' The Shreemad Bhagavatam states:

chentaḥ khalvasya bandhāya muktaye chātmano matam
guṇeṣhu sattaṁ bandhāya rataṁ vā puṅsi muktaye

(3.25.15)

'Bondage and liberation are both tied to the state of the mind. If it is attached within the three gunas, one is in bondage. And if it is detached from material things, this results in the release from maya.'

In conclusion, we must surrender our mind to God, and then we will receive His grace. To do this, let us next understand the functioning of the mind.

9

Secrets of the Mind

Mind and Brain—Same or Different

What exactly is the mind? It is a subtle piece of equipment fitted within the gross body. While science has made notable strides in comprehending the brain, the workings of the subtle mind remain a mystery. In fact, neurology is still confused whether there is a separate entity called the mind, or if the brain and the mind are the same thing.

Ancient books of wisdom explain that they are separate entities. The brain can be compared to the hardware, while the mind is the software that runs it. This explains why, even if the brain sustains damage, the mind can still function properly. The mind is made from metaphysical energy, which is subtler than the physical neurons of the brain.

The distinction between brain and mind is evident in the case of plants. Despite lacking a brain, plants exhibit signs of possessing a mind. Fascinating experiments demonstrate how plants respond to the emotions of the gardener, thereby revealing the presence of a mind in plants as well. Like plants, flatworms also do not have a brain, and yet they perform intelligent functions.

Our human mind is intensely active. It operates incessantly, producing an array of thoughts and emotions, while also serving as a repository for knowledge and memories. The thoughts we harbour create our physical and emotional personality.

Our experiences of happiness and distress are determined by thoughts. Harbouring positive emotions, such as love, sacrifice, and generosity makes us happy, while holding negative emotions, such as hatred, fear, anxiety, resentment, and jealousy makes us miserable.

Success in life is also tied to the quality of our thoughts. If we harbour noble, beautiful, and serene thoughts, our life becomes blessed. We naturally attract good opportunities and events to ourselves. In contrast, if we think selfish, violent, and dishonest thoughts, we will draw misfortune in our life.

We Are Where Our Mind Is

The mind is so powerful that it can make heaven out of hell and hell out of heaven. An uncontrolled mind can make us experience hellish torments, though we may be surrounded by heavenly luxuries. On the other hand, a trained mind can make us relish heavenly delights, even in the most hellish situations. We are literally where our mind is. Understand this through a story.

Once, a Guru asked two of his brahmachari *(celibate) disciples to purchase groceries for the ashram from the neighbouring town. They undertook the long journey. While returning, they reached a stream which was across from their ashram. The sun had set, and it was getting quite dark.*

As they were about to wade through the river, the disciples saw a young woman on the bank. She begged, 'Sirs, I am in a terrible fix. Please help me cross the stream so I may get home, else I will be stranded here for the night.'

The first brahmachari *was indignant at the request that they should carry a girl across. He walked into the water with a snort. The second* brahmachari *was more compassionate and took pity upon the helpless girl. He made her sit on his shoulders and carried her to the other side of the river. There, he set her down. She thanked him repeatedly and set off for her home, while he caught up with the first disciple whom he discovered to be in a terrible mood.*

While they continued walking towards their ashram, the first brahmachari *kept frowning and muttering to himself. An hour later, unable to hold his anger any longer, he said to his friend, 'You committed an unforgivable sin!'*

Surprised, the second brahmachari *asked, 'What sin? I have been walking silently with you.'*

'We are not allowed to touch a woman, but you carried her,' accused the first brahmachari.

With a gentle smile, the second brahmachari *said, 'I set her down one hour back, but you still seem to be carrying her in your mind.'*

Thus, in spirituality, the state of our mind is most important.

Cultivate the Garden of Your Mind

If we have a garden at home, we tend to it daily. We fertilize the soil. We sow appropriate seeds and water the plants regularly. At the same time, we are careful to weed out the wild grass as it grows faster than the plants themselves and will choke them out. If we work hard at tending our garden, it rewards us with luscious fruits and beautiful flowers. However, if we leave it to grow wild, it is quickly overrun by weeds and becomes an eyesore.

The mind, too, is like a garden given to us by God. Its fertile soil has the potential for providing us with inspiring thoughts and noble feelings. However, we have to tend to it carefully. We need to continuously fertilize it with elevating sentiments and pull out the weeds of poisonous emotions.

The mind will then reward us with a sterling and heroic character to accomplish great things. People who achieved greatness did so by cultivating their mind. The great saint Shankaracharya posed the question: *jagat jitaṁ kena?* 'Who shall conquer this world?' The wise answer he gave was: *mano hī yena* 'One who has conquered his mind'. When someone reins in and elevates their mind, their thoughts and ideas become so inspiring that they influence the entire world.

The average person's mind is not under control. Students often experience this when they sit down to study. They find their mind wandering all over the world except on the subject of study. Scientists estimate that we use less than 10 per cent of our mental and intellectual potential. The rest is dissipated because of lack of focus of the mind. Hence, we must attentively learn the fine art of controlling our mind. With this goal, let us deepen our knowledge of it.

Mind, Intellect, Chitta, and Ego

The mind has four aspects to it—mana, buddhi, *chitta,* and *ahāṅkār*. These are not distinct entities. Rather, they are four levels at which the one mind operates. Let us understand them:

1. **Mind (Mana):** When the inner machinery gives birth to thoughts, we call it mana, or the mind.
2. **Intellect (Buddhi):** When it engages in analysis and decision-making, we refer to it as buddhi, or intellect.
3. **Subconscious mind (*Chitta*):** This is the repository of memories and inner convictions. It includes impressions continuing from past lives.
4. **Ego (*Ahāṅkār*):** When it identifies with the attributes of the body and manifests pride, it is called *ahāṅkār*, or ego.

These levels of functioning are all facets of the one mind. Therefore, we can collectively refer to them in any of the following ways: the mind, or the mind-intellect, or the mind-intellect-ego, or the mind-intellect-*chitta*-ego. All these terms denote the same internal apparatus.

Various scriptures describe the mind in either of these ways, as suitable for explaining the concepts they teach. For example:

- *Panchadashi*: It refers to all four together as the mind, attributing it as the cause of material bondage.
- Bhagavad Gita: Shree Krishna repeatedly talks of the mind and intellect. He tells Arjun to surrender both to God.

- *Yog Darshan*: While dissecting the elements of nature, it mentions three entities—mind, intellect, and ego.
- Shankaracharya: In his exposition on the inner apparatus, he categorizes the mind into four divisions: mind, intellect, *chitta*, and ego.

These varying descriptions all pertain to the same inner machinery, collectively known as *antaḥ karaṇ* or the mind.

The Three Modes of Material Nature

Our mind is made from the material energy, maya. It possesses three modes: 1) sattva guna, or the mode of goodness, 2) rajo guna, or the mode of passion, and 3) tamo guna, or the mode of ignorance. The *Shwetashvatar Upanishad* of the *Yajur Veda* states:

ajāmekāṁ lohitaśhuklakṛiṣhṇāṁ
bahvīḥ prajāḥ sṛijamānāṁ sarūpāḥ
ajo hyeko juṣhamāṇo 'nuśhete
jahātyenāṁ bhuktabhogāmajo 'nyaḥ (4.5)

As per this Vedic mantra, maya is of three colours: white, red, and black. These correspond to the three gunas: sattva, rajas, and tamas. The three modes are in maya, and they are present in our mind as well. Depending upon the environment and where we focus our thoughts, one of the gunas becomes prominent. Our mind then takes on the corresponding quality.

If sattva guna dominates, one becomes peaceful, content, generous, kind, helpful, and serene. When rajo guna gains prominence, one becomes passionate, agitated, ambitious, envious of others success, and desirous for sense pleasures.

When tamo guna becomes pronounced, one is overcome by sleep, laziness, hatred, anger, resentment, violence, and doubt.

Suppose you are studying in your room. Since there is no worldly disturbance to agitate your mind, it becomes sattvic.

After finishing, you sit in your living room and switch on the television. Seeing all the imagery stimulates your mind and makes it rajasic; this intensifies your hankering for sense pleasures.

While you are watching your favourite channel, your sibling comes and changes the channel to their personal liking. This sudden disturbance causes tamo guna to develop in your mind, triggering anger within you.

In this way, our mind sways between the three gunas and takes on the corresponding qualities. Hence, our emotions fluctuate from moment to moment and from day to day. Sadhana, however, means not allowing the mind to dictate our moods. Rather, we should take charge of the mind and force it to harbour the emotions we determine are important for our well-being and growth. For this, we will have to go deeper into how the mind works, and how it can be conquered.

10

Vedic Psychology

The field of psychology explores human behaviour and the functioning of the mind. It serves as both an academic discipline and an applied science. Its various branches include psychoanalysis, psychotherapy, psychodynamics, psychiatry, and more.

Astonishingly, five millennia ago, the Vedic scriptures elucidated the science of the mind with remarkable precision. This body of knowledge, which can be termed 'Vedic psychology', eclipses the theories of modern psychology in its depth and clarity. It logically explores the origins of mental afflictions. Furthermore, it imparts valuable techniques for purifying the mind and improving our thoughts. It is comprehensively explained in the Upanishads and the Bhagavad Gita.

Exploring Vedic psychology can be a highly rewarding journey, but it requires focus and dedication. I was blessed to understand it from Jagadguru Shree Kripaluji Maharaj and am sharing the same with you here. If you carefully read the logic presented here, you will gain tremendous clarity on the workings of the mind.

Diseases of the Mind

The Vedic scriptures identify a range of human weaknesses, including anger, envy, greed, and desire, which they refer to as *mānas rog*, or mental illnesses. These afflictions are pervasive and exist as long as we remain within the realm of maya. However, the challenge lies in our limited awareness of them. While we readily admit to experiencing anger and envy, we often fail to recognize them as afflictions. Instead, we tend to dismiss them as natural tendencies. This hinders our efforts to address and remedy these issues.

We all are aware of bodily ailments and their impact on our daily life. A nagging headache or backache has the potential to disrupt our entire day. However, the detrimental effects of mental afflictions far exceed those of physical ones. Sage Tulsidas states:

eka vyādhi vaśha nara marahiñ, ye asādhi bahu vyādhi
pīṛahin santata jīva kahuñ, so kimi lahai samādhi

(Ramayan, *Uttar Kand* 7.121(A))

'Even one physical ailment is enough to incapacitate us. Then think of the plight of the soul afflicted by numerous mental ailments. Is there a means for relief?'

The power of these mental illnesses is so profound that even government laws fail to contain them. People know the consequences of violence, including potential imprisonment for life, yet they do not hesitate to transgress the law when consumed by anger. Similarly, the illegal nature of narcotics is common knowledge but ensnared in addiction many succumb to them. Why is it that we engage in behaviours harmful to the self?

To answer this question comprehensively, let us embark on a systematic exploration of these mental afflictions.

The Disease of Anger

One of the most significant mental afflictions is anger. Its emergence disrupts our inner peace. It causes a surge of blood to the head. In the aftermath of anger, we often find ourselves filled with regret over our words and actions. Later, we ponder how we allowed anger to overtake us and wish we had reacted differently.

In a quaint village lived a tailor named Suresh. He was the only tailor there and had a thriving business. Over time, Suresh became arrogant due to the villagers' reliance on his services. When people complained about his work, he would respond rudely and argue needlessly.

Despite their dissatisfaction, villagers had no choice but to visit his shop. One day, a poor woman arrived in the village. She was skilled in sewing and requested Suresh for a job, which he refused. Undeterred, she acquired a sewing machine and started her own tailoring business, offering good quality work with a friendly attitude.

Soon, most people preferred her work, and Suresh lost many customers. He became jealous and angry. His wife decided to help her husband. Without informing him, she purchased the woman's shop for one lakh rupees by convincing her that it was hard for two tailors to co-exist in such a small village. The woman gladly sold her shop and left the village that evening.

However, driven by overwhelming jealousy and anger, Suresh, under the cover of night, set fire to the woman's shop, destroying everything. His wife was aghast with disbelief when she found out the next morning and said, 'What have you done? I had already purchased her shop for one lakh rupees, on the condition that she leave the village immediately. She accepted and departed last evening itself. You have needlessly destroyed your own business and hurt yourself immensely.'

Anger erodes civility, good manners, and kindness from our behaviour. It blinds us to fundamental values of respect, empathy, and compassion. Hence, the ancient Sanskrit saying: 'Do not allow anger to overcome you; instead, become angry upon anger itself.'

The pressing question is: Why does anger arise, and is there a lasting solution to overcome it? To address this query, we must first delve into another mental affliction.

The Disease of Greed

Another pervasive mental ailment is greed. Whether it is an insatiable appetite for wealth, status, or opulent possessions, people waste their entire lives trying to satisfy their greed. However, it is impossible to fill a vessel that constantly needs more. Unlike anger, which rises and then subsides, greed never relents. The compulsion to constantly fulfill it leads to the rat race, so common in the corporate world.

Let me illustrate through a gripping story on this subject.

A sadhu once entered the court of a king. He was respectfully welcomed by virtue of his renounced status. The king asked him, 'Oh Sage, pray let me know how I may serve you.'

'Your excellency, simply fill my begging bowl with some precious stones, and then, I shall be on my way,' requested the sage.

The king summoned his treasury minister and instructed, 'Fill this monk's bowl with gold coins, gems, and precious stones.'

The minister and the king's servants began doing as instructed. To their surprise, no matter how much treasure they placed in the bowl, it remained almost empty. Overwhelmed and embarrassed, the king confessed to the sage, 'I regret I cannot fulfil my promise. I have exhausted my treasury. Your begging bowl appears to possess mystical powers. Pray, reveal its secret.'

The sadhu smiled, 'Oh King, this begging bowl is crafted from a human skull, mirroring the insatiable nature of human desires, which is to always long for more. No matter how much you fill it, it will never be satisfied.'

Such is the essence of greed—it perpetually compels us to pursue the fulfillment of desires that invariably remain elusive. The *Garud Puran* expounds:

> *chakradharo 'pi suratvaṁ suratvalābhe sakalasurapatitvam*
> *surapatirūrdhvagatitvaṁ tathāpi na nivartate tṛishṇā*
>
> (verse 2.12.14)

'A king wishes to be the emperor of the world; the emperor aspires to be a celestial god; a celestial god seeks to be Indra, the king of heaven; and Indra desires to be Brahma, the secondary creator. Yet, the thirst for material enjoyment does not get satiated.'

Greed creates the gap between what we need and what we want. In truth, we require very little to lead a content life. However, greed spawns an endless array of desires—for greater wealth, loftier positions, heightened prestige, and larger homes. The more we have, the more we crave, leaving us forever dissatisfied. Imagine the inner contentment we would be able to enjoy if only we could liberate ourselves from the clutches of greed.

Next, you will discover the origins of greed and its cure. Keep reading patiently.

The Affliction of Desire

Anger and greed are both significant mental afflictions. However, according to the Vedas, there exists an even more perilous malady, which is desire.

Desire, also known as *kāmanā*, encompasses five fundamental forms: the desire to see, hear, smell, taste, and touch. Collectively, these desires are referred to as *kām* or lust, encapsulated by the term 'desire'.

The gravity of desire is emphasized in the *Sukti Sudhakar*:

kuraṅga mātaṅga pataṅga bhṛiṅga,
mīnāhatāḥ pañchabhireva pañcha
ekaḥ pramādī sa kathaṁ na hanyate,
yaḥ sevate pañchabhireva pañcha

The verse translates as follows:

- 'The deer loves music for the pleasure of the ear. It is enticed by the hunter, who plays melodious music and shoots the deer when it comes to hear it.
- 'The elephant loves the tactile enjoyment it gets from its skin. It is allured into the net by the female elephant and

becomes easy prey for the waiting poacher.

- 'The moth lusts for the light to gratify its eyes. It is drawn to the flame and gets burned alive.
- 'The bee loves fragrance, for it gives pleasure to its nostrils. It refuses to fly off when the flower closes at sunset and gets trapped within.
- 'The fish, yearning for indulgence of its tongue, nibbles at the bait and ends up in the fisherman's frying pan.

'All these die in pursuit of the pleasure of one of the senses. What will happen to the human who chases all five objects of gratification?'

Desire stands out universally in all Vedic scriptures as the most severe mental affliction. Why is that so? Anger leads to the destruction of life and property. Greed drives individuals to waste their life in accumulating superfluous possessions. In comparison, desire appears benign in its pursuit of gratification and indulgence.

The answer is that desire is far more malevolent. It is the root cause of both anger and greed. Let us understand how.

Anger Arises from Desire

Let us learn about the origins of anger from the following narrative:

Asheesh harboured a strong craving for cake. He went to the local bakery, purchased a personal sized Black Forest cake, and carefully stored it in the fridge. To enhance his enjoyment of the treat, Asheesh decided to take a walk outdoors. Doing so would build up his appetite. His plan was to relish the cake upon his return. However, upon coming back home, he was met with disappointment—there was no cake in the refrigerator.

'I had placed a sizeable pack of cake here,' Asheesh exclaimed. 'Where could it have gone?'

'My dear husband, do you not recall?' his wife responded casually. 'The doctor had advised you to cut down on sugar. I disposed of the cake.'

'What? You threw away the cake?' Asheesh erupted in anger. His wife's action had triggered a furious outburst.

What caused Asheesh's explosive reaction? He nurtured a desire, but its fulfillment was thwarted by his wife's actions. This obstruction of desire was the catalyst for his rage. Hence, anger does not arise by itself but emerges from the hindrance of desire.

Let us explore additional examples:

- Anger often arises when we expect our family to align with our perspective, but they express contrary views.
- Anger develops when others resist following our recommendations or instructions.

Hence, desire acts as the parent, and anger is its offspring.

Sometimes, individuals approach me, 'Swamiji, I have no defect, except for anger.'

'You believe anger is your sole problem?' I inquire.

'Yes, Swamiji. Anger is my only issue.'

'That is impossible! If anger exists, its mother, desire, must also be present.'

Thus far, we have understood that the root of anger lies in the obstruction of desire. Now, let us learn how greed develops.

Greed Also Arises from Desire

Returning to Asheesh and his wife, we previously observed how Asheesh had reacted with anger on learning his wife had discarded the cake he craved.

Now, consider an alternate scenario. Suppose Asheesh's wife did not dispose of the cake. Upon his return, Asheesh eagerly indulged in it. Now, ask him, 'Did you relish the cake?'

He responds, 'Yes, I loved it!'

Inquire further, 'Then, has your desire been fully satiated?'

'No, it is merely fulfilled for today. I'll probably want it again next week.'

This illustration highlights that fulfilling desire provides only temporary relief. A while later, desire resurfaces with even greater intensity. Thus, the fulfilment of desire engenders greed.

The lesser-known truth is that desire can never be eradicated by satisfying it. It is akin to dousing a fire with clarified butter—the fire is temporarily extinguished but soon flares up with greater intensity.

Hence, like anger, greed also stems from desire. The Ramayan states: *jimi pratilābha lobha adhikāī* (*Lanka Kand* 6.101.1) 'If you satisfy desire, it results in greed.'

The Shreemad Bhagavatam states:

yat pṛithivyāṁ vrīhi-yavaṁ hiraṇyaṁ paśhavaḥ striyaḥ
na duhyanti manaḥ-prītiṁ puṁsaḥ kāma-hatasya te
(verse 9.19.13)

'If one person was to get all the wealth, luxuries, and sensual objects in the world, that person's desire would still not be satiated. Hence, knowing it to be the cause of misery, an intelligent person should renounce desire.'

In the scriptures, worldly pleasures are often likened to *mṛiga tṛiṣhṇā*, which translates to 'mirage seen by the deer'. When the sun's rays reflect on the scorching sands, they create the illusion of water. The deer, deceived by this mirage, believes there is water ahead and eagerly runs to quench its thirst. Unfortunately, its limited understanding cannot grasp that it is falling prey to an illusion. The more it chases after the mirage, the farther it recedes. Tragically, the deer keeps running for the elusive water, until it succumbs to exhaustion and dies.

Similarly, the material energy, maya, weaves an authentic-looking illusion of happiness. We find ourselves relentlessly pursuing it, hoping to satisfy the cravings of our senses. However, no matter how fervently we chase it, there is never any fulfilment.

These desires can be likened to an itch. It creates an irresistible urge to scratch. Yet, scratching it provides only temporary relief, and then, the itch returns with greater intensity. If, instead, one exercises patience and refrains from scratching, the itch gradually diminishes.

The same principle extends to the realm of desires. The mind and senses create endless cravings in the pursuit of happiness. As long as we keep fulfilling them, they continue to arise. However, when we redirect our mind away from them, we start relishing the bliss of the soul within. The *Kathopanishad* expounds on this idea, by boldly declaring that one who renounces sensual desires becomes like God:

yadā sarve pramuchyante kāmā ye 'sya hṛidi śhritaḥ
atha martyo 'mṛito bhavatyatra brahma samaśhnute

(verse 2.3.14)

'When one eliminates all selfish desires from the heart, the materially fettered atma attains freedom from birth and death and becomes godlike in virtue.' The Shreemad Bhagavatam also confirms the sublime nature of the soul devoid of cravings:

vimuñchati yadā kāmān mānavo manasi sthitān
tarhyeva puṇḍarīkākṣha bhagavattvāya kalpate (7.10.9)

'Those who eradicate wants and achieve contentment become like God.' The Bhagavad Gita also states:

vihāya kāmān yaḥ sarvān pumānśh charati niḥspṛihaḥ
nirmamo nirahankāraḥ sa śhāntim adhigachchhati (2.71)

'One who gives up all material desires and is free from greed, proprietorship, and egoism, attains perfect peace.' The elimination of desire is a central theme in Buddhist philosophy. The Four Noble Truths articulated by the Buddha are:

1) There is suffering in the world.
2) Suffering has a cause.
3) The cause of suffering is desire.
4) If desire is eradicated, suffering will be eradicated.

The cascading consequences of desire do not end with anger and greed alone. Let us explore how far this downward trajectory can extend.

Anger Destroys Good Judgement

We have observed that desire operates as a double-edged sword. Its satisfaction breeds greed, while its obstruction gives birth to anger. Once anger takes hold, it ushers in a host of other afflictions. Lord Krishna expounds in the Bhagavad Gita:

> *krodhād bhavati sammohaḥ sammohāt smṛiti-vibhramaḥ*
> *smṛiti-bhranśhād buddhi-nāśho buddhi-nāśhāt praṇaśhyati*
>
> (verse 2.63)

'Anger leads to veiling of judgement, which results in bewilderment of memory. When the memory is bewildered, the intellect gets destroyed; and when the buddhi is destroyed, one is ruined.'

The intellect serves as our internal guide. When it is obscured, we lose sight of right and wrong and get carried away by our emotions. Hence, ruin of the intellect ends in our downfall.

In this way, desire gives birth to a multitude of mental afflictions. Now, consider the reverse scenario. If we eliminate desire, greed and anger will naturally dissipate, thereby putting an end to all subsequent afflictions. We will thus gain mastery over our mind.

Given that desire is the root of these problems, let us learn what fuels desire.

The Malady of Attachment

All of us have different desires. While reading this book, one person's thoughts gravitate towards a cup of tea, while another starts contemplating cricket. Yet someone else finds the mind drifting to their child. Why do individuals generate such diverse desires?

Some people crave prestige—they go around delivering 15 lectures daily for electoral success. Others chase wealth to the detriment of their family life. Yet others are driven by the desire for a paramour, upon whom they sacrifice their hard-earned wealth. To understand this diversity, we must get to the bottom of desires.

The root of desire lies in our attachments. When our mind becomes attached to something, the fondness triggers desire. Like a magnet, attachment makes our mind cling to the object of its affection.

To illustrate, if one is attached to alcohol, thoughts of alcohol frequently occupy the mind. The fondness creates a strong desire for alcohol. Similarly, attachment to cigarettes leads to affinity for smoking and a craving for cigarettes. Thus, it becomes evident that attachment is the driving force behind desire.

This concept might appear counterintuitive. Presumably, we would think an object's inherent qualities drive our desires. However, it is not the case.

Consider the example of alcohol, which is often characterized by its foul and repulsive smell. When one takes their first sip in life, they typically find it unpleasant. However, for an alcoholic, that same disagreeable odour becomes alluring. As they pass by a pub, the whiff of whiskey makes them sway. Obviously, it is not because of the aroma, but the deep attachment to alcohol that ignites the desire.

Let us explore another example.

Is the smoke from cigarettes pleasant or repugnant? Most would describe it as terrible, something that prompts them to change their course to avoid it. So why does it hold such attraction for an addicted smoker? Once again, the power of attachment is at play. The craving for cigarettes is not driven by the intrinsic qualities of the tobacco, rather by the fondness for it in the addict's mind.

Allow me to reiterate for emphasis: **Desires arise in us not because of the intrinsic qualities of the objects themselves but because of our attachment.**

The cause of desire has now been established—attachment. The complete chain of causation is now evident. When we nurture attachment, it paves the way for desire, which, in turn, begets anger and greed. Subsequent afflictions, such as illusion and bewilderment, stem from anger. Conversely, by eradicating attachment, we eliminate the reason for desire, leading to the automatic cessation of all afflictions.

This brings us to the pivotal question: What is the source of attachment? The following section elucidates this.

The Impact of Repetitive Thinking

Attachment varies from person to person. Some are deeply

committed to their hobbies, such as gardening or golf. Others are completely attached to their spouse. Yet, others foster keenness for wealth. This variety in attachments prompts us to explore its origins.

When our intellect repeatedly contemplates happiness in an object or person, attachment takes root within us.

For instance, within a classroom, boys and girls often engage in casual interactions. However, on a particular day, one boy notices something unique about a girl. He begins to dwell on the thought, 'I would be so happy if she were my partner.'

As this idea becomes a repetitive mental pattern, his attachment to her grows. He confides in his friends, expressing an intense infatuation that is disrupting his focus on studies. His friends, who also interact with the same girl, fail to comprehend why he is so consumed by thoughts of her. The underlying reason is his persistent contemplation of finding happiness in her presence, which ultimately fosters his attachment.

Let us explore another example to illustrate the development of attachment.

How does one become attached to alcohol? It does not start with someone declaring right away, 'Fetch me a bottle! I cannot live without it.' First, friends encourage the person by saying, 'We all find great pleasure in whiskey. Why don't you also try it? Have a drink and enjoy life!'

Influenced by their misguided suggestions, he thinks, 'If my friends are enjoying it, I should too.' He takes a sip, experiencing a mental lightness as the alcohol affects his brain. This initial taste of mental numbness leads him to contemplate happiness in alcohol. Over time, as he continues to consume it, his contemplation deepens. In this way, the attachment to alcohol grows stronger, ultimately leading to addiction.

Subsequently, the individual who initially had to force himself to drink on the first day now declares, 'Just give me that fifth peg of vodka... I cannot imagine life without it!' The attachment is now so deep that he does not care about his family. He allows his business to crumble. And he is unconcerned about the state of his liver.

How did this profound transformation occur? It was a consequence of his own repetitive contemplation of happiness derived from drinking alcohol, which ultimately led to addiction.

Now, the complete chain of causation becomes evident, a concept aptly articulated in the Bhagavad Gita:

dhyāyato viṣhayān puṁsaḥ saṅgas teṣhūpajāyate
saṅgāt sañjāyate kāmaḥ kāmāt krodho 'bhijāyate (2.62)

'By repeated contemplation of happiness in the objects of the senses, one develops attachment to them. Attachment creates desire, and from desire arises anger.'

Why We All Seek Happiness

We have observed how the chain of mental afflictions commences with the contemplation of happiness. Now, let us delve into the final link in this chain. Why do we relentlessly pursue happiness? We search for it within our families, work, hobbies, activities, and all pursuits, yet it remains elusive.

Despite numerous disappointments, why do we persist in our quest for happiness?

The Vedas proclaim: *ānando brahmeti vyajānāt*, which translates to 'Know God to possess the nature of Bliss'. The Supreme Lord is an infinite Reservoir of divine Bliss, and we, as individual souls, are His fragments. Naturally, each fragment is inherently drawn towards its source. Until we attain the infinite happiness of God, our quest for everlasting joy will persist.

This means that our thirst for happiness will not cease until our soul (the part) attains the Supreme Soul (the whole). We will unavoidably envision happiness somewhere, and then, the entire chain of attachment, desire, anger, and greed will ensue.

Replace Lower Attachments with Higher Ones

The pursuit of happiness is a fundamental aspect of the soul. It is neither practical nor feasible to entirely suppress this innate drive. Instead, a pragmatic approach involves directing this yearning towards virtuous endeavours. For example, if we repeatedly associate happiness with becoming wise, we will develop a fondness for profound knowledge. This attachment, in turn, will ignite a genuine thirst for learning. It will lead to a desire for more knowledge. This will elevate and enrich our life, instead of depleting and degrading it.

Likewise, when we envision happiness in good health, we naturally develop a commitment to well-being. This desire will motivate us to become healthier.

The same principle applies to love for the Supreme. If we

consistently contemplate on the bliss of devotion to God, we will become attached to Him. The mind will then long for Him. The Shreemad Bhagavatam states:

viṣhayān dhyāyataśh chittaṁ viṣhayeṣhu viṣhajjate
mām anusmarataśh chittaṁ mayy eva pravilīyate

(verse 11.14.27)

'You repeatedly thought of the pleasures in the objects of the senses and became attached to them. Now frequently think that God is the Ocean of bliss, and you will develop devotion towards Him.'

The process remains consistent; we simply need to redirect it. The renowned Saints in history were not devoid of desire. Infact, their desire was more intense than ours. The key distinction was that while we seek worldly pleasures, they aspired to love the Lord wholeheartedly.

This brings us to the topic of God-realization. How can we attain the Supreme Divine Personality? We must now understand the various paths of yog leading to the Absolute Truth.

11

The Path of Karm

All the religions across the world emphasize a single path to God-realization. In Hinduism, however, we encounter a multitude of distinct approaches, all of which are endorsed by the scriptures. This diversity can be bewildering. Why did the Vedas not adhere to a single path?

The reason is that variety is an intrinsic aspect of God's creation. Just as no two leaves on a tree are identical and no two individuals share the exact same fingerprints, people possess diverse natures. The array of paths outlined in the scriptures caters to this inherent diversity among individuals.

As knowledge becomes more advanced and subtler, it branches out. For example, in early education, students study general science as a unified subject. Then, as they progress to higher grades, science divides into distinct disciplines, such as physics, chemistry, and biology. At the undergraduate level, these subjects further split into numerous specializations. In graduate school, the branches of science multiply exponentially.

Similarly, the Vedas expound spiritual knowledge to sublime heights. They address the diverse needs of sadhaks (spiritual aspirants) through a rich tapestry of paths. This variety is indeed a blessing.

Consider an example from the material field. When five people shop for clothing, each has their distinct preferences regarding colour and style. Likewise, in the pursuit of God-realization, the existence of various paths accommodates people with different predispositions and sanskars (tendencies from previous lifetimes). The diversity of paths serves to reach a broader spectrum of people with their unique natures and inclinations.

The Three Paths to God-realization

The Vedas refer to the Supreme as *sat-chit-anand*. These three, *sat*, *chit*, and *anand*, refer to three partitions of God's Yogmaya power.

- The nature of sat is action, or karm.
- The nature of chit is knowledge, or jnana.
- The nature of anand is devotion, or bhakti.

Hence, God has three aspects to His nature—karm, jnana, and bhakti. We souls, as fragments of God, also have the same three aspects to our nature, albeit in a far smaller measure. It is just as a drop of water has the qualities of the ocean, but to a lesser extent. Accordingly, the scriptures state the same three paths to God-realization:

yogās trayo māyā proktā nṛiṇāṁ śhreyo vidhitsayā
gyānaṁ karma cha bhaktiśh cha nopāyo 'nyo 'sti kutrachit

(Shreemad Bhagavatam 11.20.6)

'There are three paths to reach God—karm, jnana, and bhakti. No other way exists.'

The doubt that now arises is whether these three paths will take us to different goals or the same one? Do we need to participate in all three, or will any one of them suffice? Further, is there a sequence among these? For example, first do karm, then jnana, then bhakti. Or else, first do bhakti, then jnana, then karm. Or do karm, then bhakti, then jnana. This is the puzzle before us that needs to be solved.

A farmer wanted to dig a well on his property. He dug three feet in one place, and exclaimed, 'I am not getting any water here. Let me dig elsewhere.'

He dug four feet in the next place and said, 'There is a rock bed here. I will try elsewhere.'

In the third place, he dug two feet and stopped, saying, 'All I am getting here is pebbles. There is no water in this place.'

In this way, the farmer dug 50 wells, yet did not get water anywhere. However, if he had selected the right place and then continued to dig for a few hundred feet, he would have definitely found water.

Similarly, if we are perplexed about the paths to God-realization, we will keep trying different ways and reach nowhere. Hence, it is imperative to have a clear understanding about the paths to God. Let us delve into these paths, one by one. First, we will discuss the path of karm.

Duties in Life

Regardless of who we may be, there are always duties incumbent upon us. These duties safeguard us from becoming frivolous and whimsical. They ensure we learn to regulate our mind and intellect. Without them, humans would descend to the level of animals. Hinduism divides these duties into two categories—spiritual and social.

Spiritual duties: These are the duties we have towards God, Who is our eternal Father, Mother, Friend, and Well-wisher. Performing these is called bhakti, or devotion. It results in the purification of the mind and the attainment of God-realization.

The spiritual duties, or bhakti, are eternal principles that are unchanging and constant. They are also called *par dharma*, or the spiritual aspect of religion.

Social duties: When we think of ourselves as the body, we have duties towards our parents, friends and relatives, towards society at large, towards the nation to which we belong, and so forth. Performing these duties does not result in God-realization. So, these are also called *apar dharma*. However, by fulfilling them, we become responsible members of society and contribute to its overall well-being and harmony.

The social duties are often referred to as 'Karm'. They are delineated in the Vedas and are also known as 'Varnashrama Dharma'.

Varnashrama Dharma

As mentioned earlier, the social duties specified in the Vedas are called 'Karm'. These are in accordance with one's 'ashram' (stage in life) and 'varna' (occupation). They enabled society to function harmoniously, providing everyone an opportunity to fulfil their duty as per their nature, and gradually perfect their lives to attain God-realization. Some of these duties are not relevant today since the nature of society has changed. However, they helped organize Hindu society thousands of years ago, while the Western world was still dwelling in forests.

In this Varnashrama system, duties were assigned according to one's disposition and occupation, and not according to birth. The Bhagavad Gita clearly states:

chātur-varṇyaṁ mayā sṛiṣhṭaṁ guṇa-karma-vibhāgaśhaḥ

(verse 4.13)

'The four categories of occupations were created by Me, as per people's qualities and activities.'

The Vedas clearly categorize individuals into four occupational groups, not based on their birth, but by their inherent natures. This diversity in occupational choices is a universal aspect of human societies. Even in communist nations, where equality is a foundational principle, the inherent variety among individuals cannot be suppressed. In such societies too, you find philosophers serving as the intellectual backbone of the communist party, military personnel safeguarding the nation, farmers engaged in agriculture, and factory workers contributing to industrial production.

However, with time, the Varnashrama system got degraded, and the classifications became primarily by birth. This is an incorrect interpretation of the Vedas. When the British ruled Bharat, they highlighted the social practice and called it 'caste system'. Excessive publicization led to skewed understanding of Hinduism and its principles. That is why even today, in Western countries, caste system is the only thing many people know about Hinduism. They are not aware of the sublime knowledge of the science of God-realization that Hinduism teaches, which is unparalleled anywhere.

It is, thus, necessary to clarify that the Varnashrama system was not a part of the spiritual principles of Hinduism. It was a set of social duties described in Hinduism thousands of years ago. It got distorted with time, which was a social defect and Hinduism cannot be blamed for it.

This is just as slavery existed in the Western world until 200 years ago, but we do not blame Christianity, Islam, or Judaism for this social practice. In fact, even until the 1960s, discrimination on the basis of skin colour was still prevalent in the USA. It was a social ill, and we do not blame Christianity for it. Similarly, the Varnashrama system got distorted as a social ill in Bharat, and it is wrong to blame the Vedas for it.

Karm Kand—The Ritualistic Ceremonies

A part of the social duties is *karm kāṇḍ*, or the ritualistic ceremonies, which help focus the mind. Very few people have so much love for God that they can simply sit and meditate upon Him. Most people need some rituals, or ceremonial procedures, to help engage their mind positively. The Vedas describe thousands of such ritualistic practices. Some of the more popular ones are mentioned below.

Diya (lighting of the lamp). Most Hindu ceremonies commence with the lighting of a lamp which is maintained throughout the ceremony. The light of the lamp symbolizes knowledge of God, which removes the darkness of ignorance from within our hearts.

Prayer room and altar. Most homes in Bharat have a dedicated prayer room and altar on which images of God and the Guru are placed. These serve as a reminder that He is the actual Owner of the house and the Head of the family. The environment of the prayer room becomes conducive to developing sacred thoughts for worship, meditation, and devotional singing.

Aarti (ceremony of lights). With great faith and reverence, a lamp is waved around the image of God. This practice helps develop the spirit of glorifying the Lord with loving remembrance. It is often accompanied with the ringing of bells and chanting of hymns dedicated to glorifying God. This helps devotees focus on the image of God as the lamp goes around, illuminating the different parts of the deity. It is akin to open-eyed meditation on the beauty of God.

After the aarti, the lamp is offered to the devotees. They hold their hands over the flame and then place them on their eyes and head. This is a symbolic way of receiving the blessings and shakti (energy) of God.

Tilak (holy marks). God resides within everyone's heart.

Hence, the body is considered a temple of God. Holy marks are applied on the body to remind us that it is also an Abode of God, and therefore sacred. The tilak is a symbol of God and reminds us of Him.

Parikrama (circumambulating the deity). It is a way of showing respect to the deity. It also symbolizes our commitment to keep the Lord at the centre of our life as we conduct our daily duties.

Prasad (grace of the Lord). In Hinduism, food is first offered to God and later partaken as His grace. Since God is everywhere, if we offer to Him with love, He accepts. We then take the food as His remnants. This creates divine emotions within us towards the food we eat.

***Upavās* (fasting).** A great deal of our day is spent in procuring, cooking, and eating food. Fasts are suggested on certain days to reduce emphasis on eating, and instead, to dedicate that time to prayer and worship. Furthermore, occasionally eating simple food or abstaining completely benefits the digestive system, keeping it healthy.

Namaste. This is a very beautiful and sacred way of greeting each other with respect and humility. Namaste means 'I bow to the Divinity within you'. It is done with folded hands in front of the chest, to indicate reverence, and bowing of the head, to display humbleness.

There are numerous other rituals, and the essence of all is to develop divine sentiments towards God and His world.

Karm Yog—Uniting with the Supreme through Action

Karm, or social duties, help regulate the mind and elevate it to the mode of goodness. However, they cannot help us transcend maya and meet God. Thus, for genuine seekers of God-realization, there is the system of 'Karm Yog'.

'Karm' means 'work' and 'yog' means 'to unite with God'. Karm Yog is the technique of keeping the consciousness united with the Supreme while going about our daily duties. This is explained in the Bhagavad Gita:

sarveṣhu kāleṣhu māmanusmara yudhya cha (verse 8.7)

Shree Krishna says, 'Do your duty, but simultaneously remember Me at all times.'

Saints give the example of a cow. It leaves its calf in the cowshed and goes to graze grass in the fields. All day long, although chewing the cud, its mind remains in its calf.

The state of Karm Yog is an elevated one. At present, we remember God sometimes, such as when we visit the temple. However, as soon as we walk out of its precincts, we forget the Lord. To practise Karm Yog, we have to look at the whole world as His temple.

We must practise feeling the presence of God with us at all times. Jagadguru Kripaluji Maharaj emphasized it in His kirtan *Sadhana Karu Pyare*:

sochu man yah karm mam sab lakhat hari guru pyāre

(verse 32)

'Oh my mind, always remember that God and Guru are watching

all my works.' With this awareness, we will also be dissuaded from committing sins.

Live in the awareness that He is always with us as our Protector and Witness. In doing so, we will learn to execute every work as an offering unto Him. Working in such divine consciousness will motivate us to put in our best efforts. However, if the results are unfavourable, we will not feel stressed because they are not for our sake.

Shree Krishna explains this art of work:

karmaṇyevādhikāraste mā phaleṣhu kadāchana

(Bhagavad Gita 2.47)

'You have the right to do your duty, but do not be attached to the fruits of your actions.' In this way, a karm yogi practises devotion, while fulfilling social duties as well.

Let us now delve into the path of knowledge, or Jnana Yog.

12

The Path of Jnana

The Power of Knowledge

Knowledge wields great power. A person with superior knowledge can achieve in a matter of days what might take years for others to accomplish. The following example illustrates the power of knowledge.

If a small wire in an airplane gets disconnected, the airplane is unable to take off from the ground. Thousands of people work at the airport but they cannot do anything about it, and the airplane worth millions remains grounded. All it takes is one skilled aeromechanic to reconnect the wire, and the machine is ready to fly again. What does the technician have that others do not? He possesses superior knowledge about the plane's intricate machinery and functioning.

Knowledge carries the same kind of impact in the spiritual realm as well. Social scientists contend that human civilization moved from the era of agriculture to the era of manufacturing, and now it is moving towards a knowledge-based economy.

Success in any enterprise is becoming increasingly dependent upon the quality of knowledge we possess. Amazingly, 5,000 years ago, Shree Krishna had glorified the power of knowledge in the Bhagavad Gita when He told Arjun:

na hi gyānena sadṛishaṁ pavitramiha vidyate (4.38)

'There is nothing as pure in this world as true knowledge.' In the Hindu tradition, we are blessed to have a vast treasure house of knowledge available in the Vedic scriptures.

Theoretical and Realized Knowledge

While knowledge has been given such a high place in Hinduism, it has also been criticized. The *Ishopanishad* states:

andhaṁ tamaḥ praviśhanti ye 'vidyāmupāsate
tato bhūya iva tamo ya u vidyayāṁ ratāḥ

'Those who do not cultivate knowledge attain darkness. But those who go by the path of knowledge attain an even greater darkness.' Is that not surprising?! If knowledge is illuminating, how can it lead to darkness?

This is because there are two kinds of knowledge: theoretical and practical.

For example, let us say that a lady has memorized recipes in her cookbook but has never prepared food in her life. Undoubtedly, she possesses knowledge of culinary science, but it is merely theoretical knowledge. Another woman has been cooking for the last 60 years and has experienced all of its intricacies. She possesses practical knowledge of cooking. Such knowledge is far superior to mere bookish knowledge.

Similarly, in the spiritual realm, theoretical knowledge is that where one has read or even memorized the scriptures, but one has never done sadhana. On the other hand, practical knowledge is the realization one experiences upon actually surrendering to God.

Mere theoretical knowledge, which is not accompanied by practice, leads to the pride of learning. Proud people think they know, but their life does not reflect their knowledge. Hence, instead of taking them upwards in life, such knowledge can lead to downfall. Such empty and hollow learning is criticized by the scriptures. The Shreemad Bhagavatam states:

karmaṇya kovidāḥ stabdhā mūrkhāḥ paṇḍita-māninaḥ

(verse 11.5.6)

'Theoretical scholars merely learn the flowery words of the Vedas and consider themselves as pandits. But such learning, devoid of practical realization, leads to arrogance.'

In contrast, practical knowledge fosters humility. It makes us aware of our imperfections, and how much further we need to go. Such knowledge has been praised in the scriptures. In conclusion, we must 1) acquire theoretical knowledge of the scriptures, and then 2) earnestly apply the teachings in our daily life.

The next section provides a very high-level summary of the different perspectives of Indian spirituality.

Philosophical Viewpoints of Acharyas

What distinguishes *Advaita vād*, *Dvaita vād*, *Viśhiṣtha Advaita vād*, *Dvaita Advaita vād*, *Viśhuddha Advaita vād*, and *Achintya*

Bheḍābhed vād? These are the names of philosophical doctrines put forth by the founders of various traditions within Hinduism. Let us take a brief overview of them.

The *Vedant Darshan* is an important Vedic scripture, also known as *Brahma Sutra*. Great Acharyas have given their commentaries on this sacred text. The way they have explained the relationship between God, soul, and maya, has given rise to the nomenclature of their respective philosophies.

Jagadguru Shankaracharya propounded that there exists a singular entity known as Brahman. It is devoid of forms and attributes. According to his teachings, the soul is not separate from Brahman, rather, its identity is obscured by ignorance. The day ignorance is dispelled, the soul will realize itself as Brahman.

Shankaracharya further stated that maya is *mithya* (non-existent) and only seems to exist due to ignorance. Once ignorance is dispelled, maya ceases to exist. Given his emphasis on the existence of a singular entity, Shankaracharya's philosophy is termed *Advaita vād*, signifying 'Non-Dualism'.

Jagadguru Ramanujacharya accepted the existence of a single entity, Brahman, but said that it possesses diversity. He used the analogy of a tree—it contains branches, fruits, leaves, and flowers. Similarly, Ramanujacharya taught that the jiva (soul) and maya are *viśheṣhaṇ* (distinct attributes) of Brahman. Consequently, he termed his philosophy *Viśhiṣhṭa Advaita vād*, signifying 'Qualified Non-Dualism'.

Jagadguru Madhvacharya, in contrast, held an opposing perspective, emphasizing five dualities:

1. **Duality between one soul and another soul.** This is evident, when we see one soul is liberated, while another remains bound. It means they are distinct and individual.
2. **Duality between maya and the soul.** This is quite obvious too. Maya is insentient and non-conscious, while the soul possesses sentience and consciousness.
3. **Duality between maya and maya.** We consume certain foods, while considering others as inedible. This demonstrates the differentiation among items. If they were all identical, we would have no hesitation in consuming substances like mud.
4. **Duality between maya and God.** God is the omnipotent Creator, while maya serves as His energy. God is sat-chit-anand, whereas maya is devoid of consciousness. It relies on His power for its functioning. Obviously, said Madhvacharya, maya and God are distinct.
5. **Duality between the soul and God.** The soul is ensnared by maya, whereas God is the Master of maya and remains beyond its influence. The soul's knowledge is limited, whereas God possesses omniscience. The soul's consciousness is confined within a single body, while God pervades the entire universe. The soul yearns for bliss, while God is an infinite Reservoir of bliss.

Since Madhvacharya emphasized dualities, his philosophy is known as 'Dualism' or *Dvaita vād*.

Jagadguru Nimbarkacharya took a unique stance, acknowledging both 'Non-Dualism' and 'Dualism' as valid perspectives. He likened it to the relationship between a drop of water and the ocean. They can be seen as one and also as distinct entities. Similarly, the soul is a part of God, so you can either club the soul and God together and call them as one entity, or you can distinguish them and say that they are distinct from each other. Consequently, his philosophy is termed 'Dual Non-Dualism' or *Dvaita Advaita vād.*

Mahaprabhu Vallabhacharya promoted 'Pure Non-Dualism', known as *Viśhuddh Advaita vād.* He contested Shankaracharya's 'Non-Dualism', arguing that it was flawed because it negated the existence of maya and the distinct entity of the soul. According to Vallabhacharya, both maya and the soul exist, but they are one with God, resulting in what he termed 'Pure Non-Dualism' or *Viśhuddh Advaita vād.*

Chaitanya Mahaprabhu explained through the example of heat and light. He asserted that they are inherent energies of fire. Hence, heat and light are simultaneously one and different from fire. Likewise, the soul and maya are energies of God. They are simultaneously one and different from Him.

Chaitanya Mahaprabhu acknowledged that grasping the full depth of these concepts is beyond the reach of human intellect. Hence, he termed his philosophy *Achintya Bhedābhed vād*, meaning 'Inconceivable and Simultaneous Oneness and Difference'.

Jagadguru Kripaluji Maharaj, popularly known as 'Maharajji', was honoured by the Kashi Vidvat Parishat as the fifth original Jagadguru in history, and also 'Jagadguruttam', meaning 'Supreme amongst the Jagadgurus'. As a reconciler of their philosophies, He appreciated the viewpoints of all the previous

Acharyas but held the perspective of Chaitanya Mahaprabhu as dearest to Him.

Maharajji explained that the jiva and maya are both shaktis of God. All shaktis have a *bhedābhed* relationship with their *Shaktimān*. Hence, they are simultaneously one and different from Him. He emphasized selfless divine love for God as the supreme goal.

We have undertaken a whirlwind tour of the philosophical perspectives of important Acharyas. Many of the major schools of philosophy in Bharat possess their own sub-branches. For instance, within *Advait vād*, diverse viewpoints such as *Ajāta vād*, *Vivart vād*, *Avichchhed vād*, *Dṛiṣhṭi Sṛiṣhṭi vād*, and *Śṛiṣhṭi Dṛiṣhṭi vād* exist.

Additionally, there are other less popular schools of philosophy. They have used less scholasticism in presenting their respective philosophies, and hence, have not achieved recognition as a major philosophic school.

All the above philosophies can broadly be divided into two: Jnana Yog and Bhakti Yog. Let us now continue the journey by exploring the former in this chapter.

Jnana Yog

The goal of Jnana Yog is to know the 'self', or the soul. This requires analysing that one is not the body, senses, mind, intellect, or ego. Knowledge is first understood theoretically by hearing from the Guru and the scriptures. Then one repeatedly meditates on this knowledge and tries to realize it practically.

In this manner, material desires related to the body slowly diminish. Finally, one gains insight into the nature of the self. This 'self', or the soul, is a tiny part of God.

chinmātraṁ śhrī hareraṁśhaṁ sūkṣhmamakṣharamavyayam
(Vedas)

aṁśho nānā vyapadeśhāt (*Vedant Darshan* 2.3.4)

mamivāṁśho jīva-loke jīva-bhūtaḥ sanātanaḥ
(Bhagavad Gita 15.7)

īśhvara aṁśha jīva avinasī
chetana amala sahaja sukha rāsī
(Ramayan, *Uttar Kand* 7.116(B)-1)

All these verses state that the soul is a fragmental part of God. Knowledge of the self is called atma jnana, while knowledge of God is called Brahma jnana.

There exists a common misconception equating self-realization with God-realization. However, it is crucial to distinguish between these two states. At the stage of self-realization, the seeker achieves atma jnana, which is knowledge of their own soul. At the stage of God-realization, the seeker attains Brahma jnana, which is knowledge of God.

Atma jnana is only a fraction of the complete Brahma jnana. A God-realized soul undoubtedly possesses self-realization, but a self-realized soul may not necessarily have attained God-realization.

Knowledge of God, or Brahma jnana, cannot be attained by self-effort. It requires the grace of God, which must be attracted through bhakti. Shree Krishna states in the Bhagavad Gita:

bhaktyā mām abhijānāti yāvān yaśh chāsmi tattvataḥ
tato māṁ tattvato jñātvā viśhate tad-anantaram (8.22)

'Only by loving devotion to Me does one come to know who I am in Truth. Then, having come to know Me, My devotee enters into full consciousness of Me.'

Therefore, the path of Jnana Yog remains incomplete until we wholeheartedly surrender to God and immerse ourselves in His devotion. The seeker of knowledge (jnani) must engage in bhakti to invoke the divine grace of God, and then finally achieve realization of God.

Jnana Yog is Very Difficult

Even though jnana yogis finally attain God with the help of bhakti, it is a very arduous path. This is because the jnani travels a major part of the journey merely by self-effort, without the grace of God.

Understand this with the analogy of a kitten and a baby monkey. The kitten is tiny in size and delicate in build. Yet, if it is to be moved from one place to another, it need not worry. Its mother holds the kitten with her mouth and carries it around. On the other hand, a mother monkey does not take responsibility for holding the baby monkey, while she jumps from one branch to another. The baby monkey has to clasp onto the mother itself.

The path of Jnana Yog resembles the experience of the baby monkey, while the path of Bhakti Yog is like that of the kitten. The jnana yogi strives only by self-effort, without the grace of God, and thus, every obstacle becomes formidable.

gyana pantha kripana ki dhara,
parata khages hohin nahin bara

(Ramayan, *Uttar Kand* 7.118-1)

'The path of Jnana Yog is like walking on a razor's edge. It is very difficult to achieve success in it.' But the bhakti yogi surrenders to God from the beginning, and by the grace of God, is easily able to surmount hurdles on the path.

Before moving on to Bhakti Yog, let us first look at the path of Ashtang Yog, which focuses more on yogasanas and pranayam techniques to help control the mind.

Ashtang Yog

This path strives to control the mind initially with the help of physical rules and practices. The procedure consists of eight steps. Hence, it is called 'Ashtang Yog', denoting the eightfold system. They include codes of conduct, physical postures, breathing exercises, and meditation techniques. These practices help condition the body and regulate the mind and senses.

The third step amongst these is asana. It has become famous around the globe as 'yoga', and is practised for good health, beauty, and anti-ageing. Yoga studios have proliferated in cities across the world, making it a fashionable practice. However, while the postures are undoubtedly highly beneficial for physical health, the spiritual aspects are often overlooked.

The spiritual goal of Ashtang Yog is to achieve mind control. Maharshi Patanjali states in his *Yoga Sutras*:

yogaśhchittavṛittinirodhaḥ (1.2)

'The science of yog consists in the control of the workings of the mind.'

Just as in the case of Jnana Yog, Ashtang Yog also requires bhakti for its consummation. Mere self-effort is insufficient for controlling the mind. It is only when bhakti is added that it attracts divine grace and leads to true yog, or union with God. Hence the *Patanjali Yog Sutras* state:

samādhi siddhi īśhvara praṇidhānāt (2.45)

'The highest perfected state is attained by complete surrender to the Supreme.' The Ramayan states:

jogu kujogu gyanu agyanu, jahañ nahin rām prema pardhanu
(*Ayodhya Kand* 2.290.1)

'Until bhakti is added to them, Yog remains *kuyog* (not uniting), and jnana remains *ajnana* (ignorance).' The Shreemad Bhagavatam states:

tatkarma haritoṣhaṁ yatsā vidya tanmatiryayā (4.29.49)

'True knowledge is that which increases our love for God. True karm is that which is done in devotion to God.'

In this way, every path needs to be imbued with bhakti for achieving the supreme goal. The system of JKYog, incorporating yog for the body, mind, and soul teaches a perfect blend of the yogic techniques with bhakti.

So, let us now learn about bhakti, or divine love.

13

Path of Bhakti

Bhakti Yog entails the cultivation of profound love for the Divine. In bhakti, the devotee nurtures an intense yearning to behold God, to meet Him, and to remain in His presence. The mind remains firmly attached to the Supreme, and thoughts naturally flow towards Him, akin to rivers streaming into the ocean. This deep-seated love acts as a purifying force, cleansing the heart of all impurities.

With a pure heart, one begins to perceive the presence of God in all beings and in all things. As thoughts ascend to sublime heights, the devotee experiences the boundless divine bliss of God, finding complete satisfaction therein. Upon liberation, the soul does not merge with God. Instead, it ascends to His divine Abode, where it enters the *nitya leela* (blissful loving pastimes of the Lord) and engages in eternal seva.

What Is Bhakti?

Just as God is infinite, His bhakti is also infinite. So, no definition can fully encompass all the dimensions of bhakti.

Various Acharyas experienced various dimensions of it in their individual practice, and then emphasized that aspect in their definition of bhakti.

Thus, Maharishi Kapil explained, 'Just as the holy Ganga flows incessantly towards the ocean, similarly, when our thoughts begin to flow towards God, that divine state is called bhakti.' (Shreemad Bhagavatam 3.29.11)

Jagadguru Shankaracharya said, 'If needles are inserted into a potato, they remain lodged in it. Likewise, if all our thoughts are anchored in God, such a state is called bhakti.'

Jagadguru Ramanujacharya stated, 'Meditation which is endowed with love for God is bhakti.'

The *Gopal Tapaniya Upanishad* states: 'To absorb the mind in God and relish His divine Bliss is bhakti.'

Bhakti Means 'To Serve'

Sage Ved Vyas emphasized seva in his definition of bhakti:

bhaja ityeṣhavaidhātuḥ sevāyāṁ parikīrtitaḥ
tasmātsevā budhaiḥ proktā bhaktiḥ sādhanabhūyasī

(*Garud Puran*)

'The word bhakti is made from the root "bhaj", which means "to serve".'

Hence, as per Ved Vyas, bhakti is the desire to serve God. Even in the world, if we love someone, we wish to serve that person. If you say, 'I love my country', but when the time arises to defend it, you refuse to be drafted into the military, then this is not love. True love for your country should be demonstrated by your willingness to serve and protect it.

If one says, 'I love the new book that has been released,' yet confesses to not having read it even once, their professed affection is hollow. Genuine love for a book prompts an eager exploration and immersion in its pages. Similarly, **true bhakti manifests as the desire to serve and glorify God.**

Compare this with the analogy of a human hand.

As a part of the body, the hand's natural duty is to serve the body. It carries food to the mouth for feeding the body, and so on. In doing this, the hand automatically receives the nourishment, blood, and oxygen it needs for its own survival. The hand does not have to take care of itself separately. In caring for the body, the hand's self-interest is automatically met.

Now, consider a scenario where the hand refuses to serve the body, and says, 'I have had enough! All my life has passed by in serving this repulsive body. No more now! Cut me away from it, I will take care of myself.'

Do you think the hand can subsist independently? Definitely not! Its self-interest lies in serving what it is an integral part of. Likewise, the self-interest of the soul lies in serving God.

Along these lines, Chaitanya Mahaprabhu explained to Sanatan Goswami:

jīvera svarūpa haya kṛiṣhṇera nitya-dāsa

(*Chaitanya Charitamrit*, *Madhya Leela*, 20.108)

'The soul is by nature the servant of God.' Hence, devotional service to the Lord is the spiritual dharma of the soul.

Bhakti in All Aspects of Our Life

The amazing thing about bhakti is that it need not be confined to the precincts of a temple. It can be performed in any place, at any time of the day, and through any activity.

For example, let us say you are a businessman. Without bhakti, you would do business in material consciousness, driven solely by the lure for material gains. The value driving your decision is, 'Let me earn more money so that I can enjoy in the world.' However, when love for God fills your heart, your attitude transforms the same endeavour into a divine mission. Now, your overarching thought becomes, 'Let me acquire wealth so that after taking care of my bodily necessities, I can dedicate it in the service of God.'

Likewise, if you are a student, you will probably spend a large portion of your day studying. The material attitude is: 'I want good results, to get a good job, and then achieve success and riches.' However, if devotion to God becomes your motivation, the feelings towards studies will be: 'I will acquire the best knowledge by studying diligently. Then, in the future I will use my skill set to serve and please my Beloved Shree Krishna.'

Towards eating food, the material attitude is, 'Let me indulge in tasteful things and have a good time. It does not matter if my health deteriorates later, as long as I enjoy myself now.' In contrast, when your mindset gets purified with bhakti, you will still eat food but with sublime thoughts: 'Let me eat only healthy food, so I grow strong and robust, and then engage in extensive service to God.'

In this way, bhakti consecrates mundane works into sacred offerings of love.

Bhakti Can Be Done with All Materials

Bhakti is so encompassing that it can be done with anything you possess. If you have tasteful fruits, offer them to God with love and He will graciously accept them. But if no fruits are available, there is no need to worry. Offer attractive flowers to Him. If stark winter has set in and blooms are scarce, there is still no cause for concern. A handful of leaves offered with unwavering devotion will suffice. And if even leaves are not available, a simple offering of water will equally please Him.

The Bhagavad Gita says:

> *patraṁ puṣhpaṁ phalaṁ toyaṁ yo me bhaktyā prayachchhati*
> *tadahaṁ bhaktyupahṛitamaśhnāmi prayatātmanaḥ*
>
> (verse 9.26)

Shree Krishna says, 'If you offer Me with love, a leaf, fruit, flower or water, I shall accept it.' Simply remember that the whole world belongs to God, so use whatever you have to serve Him.

Bhakti Was the Basis of the Society of Bharat

In ancient Bharat, all the arts and sciences developed in the spirit of devotion to God. A majority of the ancient literature of Bharat was written on the theme of bhakti to the Lord. Spiritual fervour permeated various forms of classical Indian dances as well. Hence, dances, such as Bharatnatyam, Kathakali, and

Kuchipudi, all have devotion to the Lord as their central theme. Similarly, all the ragas (classical melodies) of Indian classical music evolved in glorification of the Supreme.

People in ancient Bharat used arts and sciences to exalt God. It was a God-centred society. This was very different from the way Western society developed. The Western world has its origins in Greek civilization. The epics of the Greeks are the Iliad and Odyssey. These are mundane stories of war and romance. In contrast, the epics of the ancient civilization of Bharat were the Ramayan and Mahabharat. Both these narratives are firmly focussed on God, replete with spiritual wisdom and instructions for spiritual growth. This spirit of bhakti reverberated through every facet of the civilization of Bharat.

The Glory of Bharat's Ancient Past

For many centuries, Bharat stood as the epitome of human civilization, firmly rooted in spirituality and God-consciousness. Unfortunately, that eminence dwindled when it became subjugated to foreign rule. Nevertheless, the splendour of its ancient past has been admired and praised by the greatest minds of the West. This is what some of them said about India:

> When India was explored and the wonderful riches of Indian theological literature found, that dispelled once and for all, the dream about Christianity being the sole revelation.[12]
>
> —Ralph Waldo Emerson, American philosopher

[12]Gokhale, Balkrishna Govind, *India in the American Mind*, Popular Prakashan, Bombay, 1992, p. 344.

If I were to look over the whole world to find out the country mostly richly endowed with all the wealth, power, and beauty that nature can bestow—in some parts a very paradise on earth—I shall point to India. If I were asked under what sky the human mind has most fully developed some of its choicest gifts, has most deeply pondered on the greatest problems of life, and has found solutions of some of them...I shall point to India. And if I were to ask myself from what literature we, here in Europe,...may draw that corrective which is most wanted in order to make our inner life more perfect, more comprehensive, more universal, in fact more truly human,...again I shall point to India.[13]

—Professor Max Müller, German orientalist, considered the father of comparative religion

If there is a country on earth that can justly claim the honour of having been the cradle of the human race, or at least the scene of human civilization, the successive developments of which carried it into all parts of the ancient world, and even beyond, the blessings of knowledge, which is the second life of man, that country is assuredly India.[14]

—Friedrich Creuzer, German philologist and archaeologist

---

[13]Müller, F. Max, *India: What Can It Teach Us, A Course of Lectures Delivered Before the University of Cambridge*, Longmans, Green, and Co., London, 1883, p. 6.

[14]Lal, Chaman, *India: Mother of Us All*, Bhikshu Chaman Lal, New Delhi, 1968, p. 24.

> This is indeed India!...cradle of the human race, birthplace of human speech, mother of history,...the one land that all men desire to see, and having seen once by even a glimpse, would not give that glimpse for the shows of all the rest of the world combined.[15]
>
> —Mark Twain, American writer

> Powerful empires existed and flourished here while Englishmen were still wandering painted in the woods, and when the British Colonies were wilderness and jungle; and India has left a deeper mark upon the history, the philosophy, and the religion of mankind than any other terrestrial unit in the universe.[16]
>
> —Lord Curzon, Viceroy and Governor General of India from 1899–1905

Having discussed the glory of devotion in this chapter, we will now move on to learn how to develop devotion in our heart.

---

[15]Twain, Mark, *Following the Equator – A Journey around the World*, 1897, http://tinyurl.com/bp5ztp78. Accessed on 5 February 2024.

[16]*Speeches by Lord Curzon of Kedleston, Viceroy and Governor General of India. Vol. III. 1902–1904*, Office of the Superintendent of Government, Calcutta, 1904, p. 99.

14

The Three Manifestations of God

When we desire to engage in bhakti, the first question that arises is: 'Which Form of the Supreme should I worship?' We have many options in Hinduism so deciding which Entity to worship requires knowledge of the various aspects of God's personality.

Three Ways in Which the Supreme Entity Manifests in the World

Picture yourself standing beside a railway track. In the distance, you spot the headlight of an approaching train, resembling a radiant light. As the train draws nearer, its luminosity assumes a discernible form. Finally, when it stands before you, the realization dawns: 'Ah, it is a train! I can even see the passengers peering out of their windows.'

The train seemed like a light from afar. As it came closer, it appeared to have a shimmering form. Finally, when it came right in front, you realized it was a train. The train was the same—as its proximity increased, your understanding of its passengers, compartments, doors, and windows grew. Likewise, the Supreme Divine Personality can be realized in varying degrees of closeness.

God is perfect and complete and the possessor of unlimited energies. Hence, His personality is replete with divine Names, Forms, Pastimes, Virtues, Associates, and Abodes. Yet, He is realized at different levels of proximity as Brahman, Paramatma, and Bhagavan. The learned Sage, Ved Vyas writes:

vadanti tattattva vidastattvaṁ yajgyānamadvayam
brahmeti paramātmeti bhagavāniti śhabdyate

(Shreemad Bhagavatam 1.2.11)

'The Supreme Lord manifests in this world in three ways: Brahman, Paramatma, and Bhagavan.' These are not three different Gods, rather they are three manifestations of the same one God. However, they exhibit dissimilar qualities. Compare this to H2O (water).

Water, steam, and ice are the same substance, but their physical qualities are not alike. If a thirsty person asks for water, and you give her a lump of ice, she will say, 'What is this? I asked for water.'

You may tell her, 'Since ice is made from H2O molecules, it is the same as water.'

She will reply, 'It is the same substance, but its physical properties are different. I cannot drink ice. It will not quench my thirst.'

Likewise, Brahman, Paramatma, and Bhagavan represent different manifestations of the one Supreme Lord, but Their qualities are different.

Brahman

This is the aspect of God that is everywhere in creation. The Vedas state:

eko devaḥ sarvabhūteṣhu gūḍhaḥ
sarvavyāpī sarva bhūtāntarātmā

(*Shwetashvatar Upanishad* 6.11)

'There is only one God. He is seated in everything and in everyone.' As Brahman, God does not manifest His Forms, Virtues, and Pastimes. He is merely *sat-chit-anand*, meaning 'full of eternality, knowledge, and bliss'.

You may wonder that if God is everywhere, why can we not perceive Him? The reason is that He is divine, while our senses are all made from the material energy. Consequently, these material senses cannot comprehend Him. The following story amply illustrates it.

An ant kept a lump of salt in its mouth and climbed up a hill of sugar. Another ant accompanied this ant up the hill. In the evening when they returned, the second ant said, 'Today I ate so much sugar that I am stuffed with it.'

The first ant exclaimed, 'What are you saying, my dear friend? We walked on a hill of salt. How did you get to eat sugar?'

The first ant's statement may seem surprising. If they were walking on a hill of sugar, how come the first ant did not experience it? The answer will become evident if you open its mouth. Inside was a lump of salt that prevented it from tasting the sweetness of sugar.

Similarly, God pervades all of creation as the Formless Brahman. However, our senses are material, and hence, we are unable to perceive Him.

The path of Jnana Yog takes us to the realization of the all-pervading Brahman, devoid of attributes. This is a distant realization of God as a bright Light, just as the train from afar appeared to be like a light.

Paramatma

This aspect of God resides in the heart of all beings. This means that there are two personalities residing in the body—the atma (individual soul) and the Paramatma (Supreme Soul). The Bhagavad Gita states:

īśhvaraḥ sarva bhūtanaṁ hṛiddeśhe 'rjuna tiṣhṭhati (18.61)

Shree Krishna says: 'Arjun! God resides in the heart of all living beings.'

Seated within our heart, the Paramatma meticulously observes all our thoughts and actions, keeps an account of them, and dispenses the results at the appropriate time. While we may forget our past actions, God has perfect recollection. If you were asked, 'What were you thinking 25 hours and 15 minutes ago?', you would probably say, 'I do not remember.' However, God remembers what we thought at every moment of our life since we were born.

And not only for this life! Through endless lifetimes, wherever we went, God remained our constant Companion. This manifestation of God dwelling in everyone's hearts is the Paramatma. We can refer to Him as the Supreme Soul within.

He possesses a Form and Virtues. However, He does not display any Pastimes.

The path of Ashtang Yog focuses on God residing in the heart and takes us to the Paramatma realization. This is a closer experience of the Supreme Entity, just as the train was seen as a shimmering light form as it drew nearer.

Bhagavan

This is the aspect of God when He takes on a personal Form. The Shreemad Bhagavatam states:

kṛiṣhṇamenamavehitva mātmānamakhilātmanām
jagaddhitāya so 'pyatra dehīvābhāti māyayā (10.14.55)

'The Supreme Lord—who is the Soul of all souls—manifested in His personal Form, as Shree Krishna, for the welfare of the world.' We refer to the personal form of God with the nomenclature 'Bhagavan' or 'Avatar'.

As Bhagavan, He reveals the sweetness of His Names, Forms, Qualities, Abodes, Pastimes, and Associates. Do note that Bhagavan is not bigger than Paramatma, nor is Paramatma bigger than Brahman. They all are the same Supreme Divine Entity. All the attributes of Bhagavan also exist in Brahman and Paramatma, but some remain dormant.

Compare this to a matchstick. It contains fire in the latent form. The fire manifests when the matchstick is struck against the igniting strip of the matchbox. Similarly, all the qualities of God's personality, which are latent in the other forms, get revealed in His Bhagavan manifestation.

The path of Bhakti Yog leads to the attainment of Bhagavan.

This is the closest realization of God. It is akin to the details of the train becoming visible when it comes and halts in front of the observer. In essence, bhakti allows one to perceive and embrace the personal and intimate aspect of the Divine. The Bhagavad Gita states:

bhaktyā māmabhijānāti yāvānyaśhchāsmi tattvataḥ
tato māṁ tattvato gyātvā viśhate tadanantaram

(verse 18.55)

Shree Krishna says: 'Only by loving devotion to Me does one come to know who I am in Truth. Then, having come to know Me, My devotee enters into full consciousness of Me.'

The Bliss of the Personal Form of God

Many people choose to worship the Supreme as the all-pervading Brahman. Others prefer to connect with Him in any of His personal Forms, such as Bhagavan. The bliss of the Formless is called *brahmanand*, while that of His personal Form is called *premanand*. Both are infinitely sweet. And yet, there is a distinction between them that needs to be understood.

Let us say, the husband of a married woman prohibits her from seeing him. He also never allows her to serve him, speak to him, or love him. Would that wife not find her life exceedingly dull? She would say, 'I longed for a husband with whom I could sing, dance, play, and love. Instead, I have married a bore.'

Likewise, those who worship the formless Brahman cannot see their Lord; they cannot witness His sweet Leelas; they cannot hear the melodious sound of His flute; they have no opportunity to feel the love of His embrace. They can only experience Him in their minds. In contrast, the devotees of Bhagavan behold the divine Form of their beloved Lord, engage in His sweet Pastimes, and serve Him to their heart's content.

Do note that both *premanand* and *brahmanand* are sweet, yet one is sweeter. *Compare this with jaggery, sugar, and candy. They are all sweet. However, if you were eating jaggery, and someone put candy in front, you would lose interest in jaggery. The jaggery is sweet, but sugar is sweeter, and candy is the sweetest.* Consider another example to understand this point.

Suppose a woman is carrying a baby in her womb. Although she has not yet seen her baby, the anticipation of becoming a mother brings her joy. After the baby is born and begins to grow, the mother cherishes the moments of holding her two-month-old baby in her lap with great love. Ask that mother, 'The joy you are experiencing from your baby now, is it the same as the joy you got when the baby was in your womb?'

The mother will say, 'What are you saying? Pregnancy was nine months of sheer pain; it was just a feeling of the baby inside. But now I can see my little daughter, hug her, hear her childish chatter, enjoy her innocent pastimes, and serve her. This is real bliss.'

Similarly, worshipping the formless Brahman simply gives a feeling of bliss in the mind. In contrast, in the worship of Bhagavan, we experience all the sweetness of His Names, Forms, Qualities, Pastimes, Abodes, and Associates.

Further, worship of the personal Form of God is easier as well. If you were asked to watch and think about a light for six hours, the task may prove to be challenging. However, if you are made to see a wonderful drama, with a great story, attractive actors, and lots of action, it would be enjoyable and effortless. Similarly, the variety of the attributes of Bhagavan makes devotion to Him considerably easier and more fulfilling.

When we wholeheartedly engage in devotion, placing our faith in the divine nature of God's Forms and Pastimes, our mind undergoes rapid purification.

Various Personal Forms of God

In the Hindu tradition, we are fortunate to possess knowledge about the diverse personal Forms of God. In these forms, He eternally exists in His divine Abodes. Occasionally, He descends on earth as an Avatar and displays His divine Leelas.

These loving Pastimes of God have been documented in the scriptures and related by the Saints. Some of the prominent Forms of God described in the Vedic scriptures are:

Shree Krishna. He resides eternally in His divine Abode, which is called *Golok*. Shree Krishna descended on the earth about 5,000 years ago and displayed sweet loving Pastimes that have enchanted billions of people since then. Notably, Shree Krishna is also the speaker of the Bhagavad Gita. His Leelas have been vividly described in the Mahabharat and in the tenth canto of the Shreemad Bhagavatam.

Shree Krishna's threefold bending posture adorned with a peacock crown, His bluish complexion, and the enchanting melody of His flute, have captured the imagination of hundreds of thousands of poet-saints. In His loving Pastimes, Shree Krishna demonstrated how He willingly becomes enslaved by the love of His devotees', even forgetting that He is God.

Shree Ram. His eternal Abode is called *Saket Lok.* He descended on the earth in the *Tretā Yug.* Bhagavan Ram set an impeccable example of perfect behaviour for human beings. He was the ideal Son, the ideal Brother, ideal Friend, and ideal King. Human society derives great inspiration from the way He discharged His social responsibilities.

Lord Ram's captivating Form and remarkable Pastimes irresistibly enchant the minds of devotees. One of His most enduring Leela's is His vanquishing of Ravan, the demon king, to rescue Mother Sita from captivity. These extraordinary Pastimes were described by the ancient poet Valmiki in his great Sanskrit work, the Ramayan, and later translated into numerous regional languages across Bharat.

Lord Vishnu. He oversees the administration of the material worlds. Vishnu Bhagavan rests upon the body of Anant Shesh, the divine snake-form of God. Simultaneously, He also resides in everyone's heart as the Paramatma.

His eternal Abode in the divine realm is known as *Vaikunth,* where He resides as Lord Narayan. He has a four-armed form with a conch shell, disc, lotus flower, and mace, in His hands. However, He rarely performs any Pastimes. Mother Lakshmi is His eternal consort. In South India, He is commonly referred to as Lord Venkateshwar.

Bhagavan Shiv. He resides in the divine realm as *Sadashiv* and in the material realm as Bhagavan Shankar. He exudes an aura of profound tranquillity, and remains in deep meditation in His abode, called *Kailash.* Known for His boundless compassion and mercy, Shivji gives shelter to even the lowest of sinners and drunkards.

When the time arrives for the dissolution of the universe, He initiates His famous *Tāṇḍav* dance and winds up all of creation. Mother Parvati is His eternal consort. Shiv and Parvati's divine Pastimes are mentioned in many of the Puranas, especially in the *Shiv Puran*.

Mother Durga. She is in charge of the functioning of the material energy. Hence, She is worshipped as the Divine Mother of the world and of all the souls residing in the material realm.

The worship of God in the form of the Mother is a remarkable aspect of Hinduism. Just as a child believes its mother to be all-powerful and immensely kind-hearted, likewise, a devotee believes the Divine Mother to be infinitely merciful, all-powerful, and eternally protective with Her invisible arms.

Radha Rani. The divine energy of God manifests in various Forms, such as Radha, Durga, Kali, Lakshmi, Parvati, Sita, and Rukmini. They all are revered as the Divine Mother of the universe. The motherly aspect of God emanates beauty, gentleness, kindness, and tenderness. The sweetest Form of the Divine Mother is Radha. She is the divine energy of Shree Krishna. By Her power, *Shyamsundar* (Krishna) manifests His amazing Pastimes, divine Abode, and divine Bliss.

Radha Rani's boundless selfless love makes Her the foremost devotee in Shree Krishna's divine Leelas. By Her grace, souls are blessed with pure love for *Shyamsundar* and His loving service.

Ganesh. Revered as the remover of obstacles, He holds a special place in Hindu religious ceremonies. Ganeshji is invoked at the outset of auspicious endeavours as *Vighneshwar*, the dispeller of impediments. He is also the bestower of knowledge, hence is also called *Vinayak* (knowledgeable). In his divine Pastimes, Ganesh is the younger son of Lord Shiv and Mother Parvati. With four hands, an elephant's head, and a generous belly, his unique form embodies His magnanimous nature.

Hanuman. He is a great devotee, epitomizing unwavering devotion to Lord Ram. Hanumanji is endowed with exceptional heroic qualities. He sets an excellent example of renunciation and austerity, serving as an ideal for all who seek inspiration from His remarkable pastimes.

Hanumanji's love for Shree Ram is immense, and while serving, He does not hesitate to undertake the most herculean tasks. He carries a *gadā* (mace), representing His valour and heroism.

We shall now discuss how to engage in devotion to achieve the highest level of God-realization, and also experience *premanand*, the bliss of divine love.

15

Divine Love—The Greatest Treasure

The Powers of God

All of us possess a multitude of powers, including the ability to see, hear, and think. We need numerous powers to accomplish any task. If even one power reduces, we become handicapped. For example, if a man says, 'I am blind,' it means his power to see is missing.

God possesses innumerable powers, and each is unlimited in extent. Hence, He is called *Sarva-śhaktimān*. One of God's powers is maya, the material energy, with which He creates the material world. If we carefully ponder over even a speck of this amazing creation, we can perceive the miracle of God manifesting in it. Keep in mind that all this has come about by God's most inferior energy, maya.

Beyond this, He possesses a superior spiritual power, called Yogmaya. With the help of Yogmaya, the Lord manifests His divine Abodes, Forms, Virtues, and Pastimes. Imagine, if maya shakti is so astonishing, how magnificent and glorious will be the works of Yogmaya! The divine Leelas that Shree Krishna, Shree Ram, and other Avatars performed were all by virtue of this Yogmaya power.

Yogmaya has many branches. One of them is *Hlādini shakti,* the power that gives pleasure to God. The quintessence of this power is *para bhakti,* or divine love. It is the most confidential of His powers. Let us delve into its secrets.

The Power of Divine Love

This is God's most extraordinary power. It is so special that the Supreme Almighty becomes a servant of the devotee who possesses bhakti. The Shreemad Bhagavatam states:

ahaṁ bhaktaparādhīno hyasvatantra iva dvija
sādhubhi rgrastahṛidayo bhaktairbhaktajanapriyaḥ (9.4.63)

Shree Krishna states: 'I am supremely independent, but divine love is such a power that it binds Me. My devotees who possess it rule My heart and are very dear to Me.'

Whenever God descends in this world, He reveals loving Pastimes, in which He shows how He is enraptured by the love of His devotees. There are innumerable verses to this extent:

vyāpaka brahma nirañjana nirguna vigat vinoda
so aja prema bhagati basa kausalyā keñ goda

(Ramayan, *Bal Kand* 1.198)

Sage Tulsidas states: 'We all know that God is all-pervading in this world. We also know about His formless aspect. However, look at the power of Kaushalya's bhakti, under whose spell, the very same Supreme Lord has become a small Baby and is lying in her lap.'

Jagadguru Shree Kripaluji Maharaj described how God gets enchanted by bhakti:

jo nahiñ jāta bulāyehu śhuka sanakādika dhyāna
binuhiñ bulāye jāta soi ghara ghara braja vanitāna

(*Bhakti Shatak* verse 93)

'Look at the glory of divine love. The Supreme Master of infinite universes, Who hesitates to reveal Himself in the samadhi of great personalities like Shukadev and Sanatkumar goes uninvited to the houses of the gopis of Braj.'

The profoundly captivating Leelas depicted by the preceding verses reveal that God is captivated by the power of divine love. A very endearing Pastime of the Lord illustrating this point is described below.

The Supreme Personality Gets Tied by a Rope

When Shree Krishna descended on the earth, despite being the Lord of all the worlds, He assumed the form of a little child, frolicking with His cowherd friends and stealing butter from the gopis.

Once when Shyamsundar was a toddler, Mother Yashoda was churning butter in the kitchen. Although with her hands she was pulling the rope, her mind was absorbed in loving thoughts of Krishna. 'Let me churn very soft and sweet butter', she was thinking, 'so that I may feed my Krishna with it. He loves butter and eating the freshly churned butter will make Him very happy indeed.'

Shree Krishna reached the scene. Finding His mother engrossed in churning butter, He sought her affectionate attention. He climbed onto her lap, caught her face with His tiny hands, urging her to look in His direction. Observing her dear Krishna's naughtiness gave great pleasure to Mother Yashoda. She began feeding Him milk with immense love. Krishna was enjoying His mother's affection.

In the meantime, the milk that had been set to boil started spilling over. Seeing this, Yashoda hastily put Krishna aside and rushed to take the milk off the fire.

Krishna was annoyed that His mother left Him to tend to the milk, as if it were more important than Him. To express His displeasure, He took the churning rod and smashed the pot of butter. He also broke some more pots nearby. Then, He carried a small pot of butter out of the house. He ate some butter Himself and began feeding the rest to the monkeys.

Having taken care of the milk, Mother Yashoda returned to the butter. She was startled to see all the pots smashed. She decided to teach her child a lesson, so taking a stick in her hands, she ventured out of the house.

Finding His mother so angry, Krishna ran to save Himself from a beating. His four steps were equal to one of Yashoda's. However, He was still swifter than His mother, and as the chase continued, she became increasingly tired.

The Lord is faster than the fastest, so who can ever catch Him?

Seeing Yashoda's exhaustion, Krishna felt pity for her and pretended to get tired Himself. He slowed down, allowing Mother Yashoda to catch Him. God is the Father of all souls, but because of Yashoda's love, He subjected Himself to the role of her Child.

The mother has the right to punish her child for his betterment, and so Yashoda took a rope to bind Krishna to the grinding wheel. However, the rope turned out to be two fingers short. So, Yashoda tied a second rope to the first one and again tried to bind Krishna. But again, the rope was two fingers short! No matter how many ropes Yashoda kept adding, the rope was still not long enough to tie Krishna. God is bigger than the whole universe, which resides inside Him. Unless He himself permits it, who can ever tie Him?

Mother Yashoda was bewildered! Finally, Krishna again felt pity on her and allowed Himself to be tied. The scriptures state:

yaśhodayā samākapi devatā nāsti bhūtale
ulūkhale yayā baddho muktido muktimichchhati

'Can any celestial god be as fortunate as Mother Yashoda? That Lord, who releases the souls from the bonds of maya, has been tied by her with a rope. He is begging her for His release.'

This amazing Pastime reveals the glory of divine love and shows how the devotee can bind the Supreme Lord simply with love.

The Greatest Treasure We Can Possess

God happily serves that devotee who possesses the treasure of divine love. This is why, in the Mahabharat war, Shree Krishna drove the chariot, while Arjun merrily sat on it. Shree Krishna is the Supreme Master of the universe, while Arjun was a mere soul. And yet, because of Arjun's devotion, Shree Krishna took the subservient position of being his Charioteer.

This is the glory of divine love, in front of which all worldly opulences become insignificant. While material treasures will remain behind when we depart from the world, the treasure of divine love will accompany us beyond death. Thus, it is the highest treasure that we can possess. Saint Kabir said:

kabīrā saba jaga nirdhanā dhanvañtā nahiñ koya
dhanvañtā soi jāṇiye jāhi prema dhana hoya

'Nobody in this world is really wealthy, except that person who possesses the wealth of divine love.'

We must now try to find out how we too can receive this priceless treasure.

16

Sadhana Bhakti—Preparatory Devotion

God does not bestow *para bhakti* easily, for doing so will entail becoming enslaved by the devotee. He waits till the soul becomes deserving of it. If we wish to receive it, we will have to qualify for it. The criterion is the preparation of the *antaḥ karaṇ* (ethereal heart).

We must purify our mind completely until it becomes a suitable receptacle for *para bhakti*. We all are aware of the importance of keeping our home clean. If we wish to invite an esteemed person to our home, we will first clean and tidy the house. Instead, if we have a dead dog lying on our living room carpet, our guest will depart in a hurry, saying, 'What an awful place! The stink is unbearable. Please invite me later when you have perfectly cleaned up your house.'

Likewise, a temple is first cleaned and then the deity of the Lord is installed in it. Similarly, *para bhakti* is like a maharani (queen). If we desire the queenlike divine love to reside in our heart, we must first make it pure.

Jagadguru Shree Kripaluji Maharaj explained in *Bhakti Shatak*:

prathama sādhanā bhakti karu, taba mana nirmala hoya
milai viśhuddhā bhakti taba, guru anukampā ṭoya

(verse 9)

'First, do *sadhana bhakti* to purify your mind. Then you will receive *siddha bhakti* by the grace of the Guru.'

Preparatory Devotion

How will the mind be cleansed? This will happen by engaging in *sadhana bhakti*, or 'preparatory devotion'. It will prepare the vessel of the heart, in which God will then bestow *siddha bhakti*, which is His divine love.

Hence, bhakti is of two kinds:

1. **Preparatory devotion**, or *sadhana bhakti*, is what we have to do. It is the effort required from us for cleansing the mind of anger, greed, lust, envy, pride, and illusion.
2. **Divine Love**, or *siddha bhakti*, is the divine power that God bestows by His grace.

Purification of the mind is a natural consequence of *sadhana bhakti*. God is all-pure; He is beyond the three gunas of maya. When we attach our mind to Him, it gradually rises above the three modes. Initially, tamo guna, the mode of ignorance, is extinguished. Then, rajo guna, the mode of passion, is eliminated, and the mind becomes established in sattva, the mode of goodness. Finally, by the grace of God, sattva guna is also destroyed, and the mind is made divine. At this stage, *sadhana bhakti* is complete, and the vessel is ready for receiving *siddha bhakti*.

Therefore, let us first learn how to do preparatory devotion. The first point in *sadhana bhakti* is to develop our relationship with God.

Our Eternal Relationship with God

Our deepest and most comprehensive relationship in the world is with the Lord. Physically, He is so close to us that not a hair's breadth gap exists between Him and us. He is seated within us, and we are seated within Him. The *Kathopanishad* states:

nityo nityānāṁ chetanaś chetanānām (2.2.13)

'God is seated within the soul, bestowing it eternality and life.' If He were to leave us for a moment, our soul itself would cease to exist.

Therefore, God is our eternal Relative. The worldly relatives keep changing from lifetime-to-lifetime. In our previous birth, we had a different father, mother, sister, brother, and friends. In the birth before that, we had another set of relatives. God, however, is our eternal Father, Mother, Friend and Relative. In endless lifetimes, wherever we went, God went with us. When we went into a cat's body, God accompanied us. When we went into a cow's body, God went with us there as well.

The Bhagavad Gita states:

gatir bharta prabhuh sakshi nivasah sharanam suhrit
prabhavah pralayah sthanam nidhanam bijam avyayam

(verse 9.18)

Shree Krishna says, 'I am the Supreme Goal of all living beings, and I am also their Sustainer, Master, Witness, Abode, Shelter, and Friend. I am the Origin, End, and Resting Place of creation; I am the Repository and Eternal Seed.'

Further, He is such a Friend Who is totally selfless. Since He is perfect and complete, He needs nothing from us. Hence, He always desires and acts for our welfare. This is a stark contrast from worldly relatives whose love for us is tinged with selfishness.

Thus, God is both our eternal and selfless Friend. The problem, however, is that we have forgotten our relationship with Him since innumerable lifetimes. So, effort will be required to remember and re-establish it.

The Need to Rekindle Our Relationship

Suppose you had a friend who was very close to you in college. Upon graduation, life took you both in different directions, so you lost contact. Now you meet her after a gap of 15 years. You try to greet her by hugging her and say, 'Anita! What a pleasure to meet you after so long!'

Your friend, however, failed to recognize you. She looks at you in puzzlement. 'Who are you?' she asks.

'You did not recognize me? We used to study together in college.'

'Oh yes! I have a faint recollection.'

'Sometimes we would go biking together!'

'Yes...yes, I am remembering more now.'

'We specialized in the same major. And we were in many classes together.'

'Oh yes, now I remember! You are Sheila.'

We see how Anita was a friend of Sheila, but she had forgotten, and so she required some effort to remember.

Similarly, we too have forgotten our Eternal Relative. So, we will require some effort to rekindle that divine relationship. That is what *sadhana bhakti* will help us do.

The Five Bhavs of Bhakti

Another name for bhakti is *upāsanā*. The word *upāsanā* means to come close to God. How can we do that? By thinking, 'He is mine'. We can enhance our love for God by establishing sweet loving relationships with Him.

There are five bhavs (sentiments) of devotion towards the one Almighty Lord. These are the five ways for taking our mind to Him. They have been detailed in the various bhakti scriptures, such as the *Narad Bhakti Darshan*, the *Bhakti Rasāmṛit Sindhu*, *Prema Rasa Siddhanta*, and so on. The five bhavs are:

1. ***Śhānt bhav*, or the sentiment of Majesty:** 'The Lord is my King.' For example, the residents of Dwarika saw God as their King, Dwarikadhiṣh. The residents of Ayodhya saw Bhagavan Ram as their King.
2. ***Dāsya bhav*, or the sentiment of Servitude:** 'God is my Master.' Hanuman is the supreme ideal of this bhav towards His Master, Shree Ram.
3. ***Sakhya bhav*, or the Fraternal sentiment:** 'God is my

Friend.' This was the sentiment of Arjun. Shree Krishna's cowherd friends also loved Him in *sakhya bhav*.

4. ***Vātsalya bhav*, or the Maternal sentiment:** 'I am Shree Krishna's mother or father.' This was the sentiment of Yashoda towards Krishna. It was also the sentiment of Kaushalya towards Ram.
5. ***Mādhūrya bhav*, or the Conjugal sentiment:** 'Shree Krishna is my Beloved.' This is how the gopis of Vrindavan worshipped Shree Krishna. Meera Bai exemplified this bhav (sentiment of devotion). She looked upon the Lord as her Beloved, and thereby, felt the greatest proximity with Him.

These sentiments help us get closer to God. Devotion may sometimes resemble worldly love, but actually it is totally the opposite. The distinction is that love in the world is selfish, while true love for God is completely selfless. We shall learn about selfless love in the next chapter.

17

Selfless Love

Do Not Ask God for Worldly Things

If we approach God with worldly desires, our mind remains entangled in the world. Then no matter how much devotion we do, the mind does not become pure. It is like filling dirty water in a bottle and submerging it in the holy Ganga. Regardless of how long the bottle remains immersed in the sacred river, the water within stays impure. This is because it did not come in contact with the pure water of the Ganga.

In a light-hearted tale, two neighbours, Ramesh and Dinesh, fell victim to the classic trap of neighbourly envy. Their rivalry led to an endless cycle of mimicking each other's choices, from buying new cars to building fences and repainting their houses.

Years passed, and their feud made them unable to stand each other's presence. To outdo Dinesh, Ramesh hatched a plan. He decided to seek a boon from Bhagavan Shiv. The next morning at 5.00 a.m., he arrived at the temple and began chanting 'Om Namah Shivaya', vowing not to stop until Lord Shiv appeared to fulfil his wishes.

Coincidentally, Dinesh had the same idea the previous night—to surpass Ramesh by seeking a boon from Lord Shiv. At 5.15 a.m., he reached the same temple and spotted Ramesh meditating there. He realized his intentions and thought, Let us see who receives a boon from Bhagavan Shiv first. He too began chanting.

Around 7.00 a.m., devotees arriving at the temple observed Ramesh and Dinesh, apparently in deep devotion. It seemed to them that both were remarkably devout souls.

At noon, Mother Parvati suggested to Lord Shiv that He visit Ramesh and Dinesh. Shivji appeared before Ramesh, who inquired whether Dinesh had received the Lord's darshan yet. Shivji responded that He would visit Dinesh next.

Hearing this, Ramesh faced a dilemma. Whatever he asked for, Dinesh would request more of the same. So, he cunningly said, 'Oh Lord, grant me double of whatever You bestow to Dinesh.'

Shivji then approached Dinesh, who similarly inquired about Ramesh's darshan. Upon discovering that Ramesh had indeed met Lord Shiv, Dinesh found himself in a predicament. Despite his rigorous penance, he would still lag behind Ramesh. Ultimately, he sought an advantage by asking Shiv to make him one-eyed.

Lord Shiv granted Dinesh's unusual boon, rendering him one-eyed, while Ramesh was left completely blind. The devotees, who had initially believed the two men to be devout, soon realized that their minds were firmly entrenched in worldly desires despite their vocal prayers to God.

If, externally, we worship the Lord, but our mind clings to material desires, it will be devotion to the world, not to God.

Such bhakti will not cleanse the mind from the afflictions of maya.

The scriptures label this type of bhakti as *sakām* bhakti. **If we wish to purify our mind, we must learn *nişhkām* bhakti, in which we do not ask God for anything.** This is the instruction of all the Vedic scriptures. The Shreemad Bhagavatam states:

lakşhaṇaṁ bhakti-yogasya nirguṇasya hy udāhṛitam
ahaituky avyavahitā yā bhaktiḥ puruşhottame (3.29.12)

'Devotion to the Supreme Divine Personality should be untinged by material aspirations; it should flow without any interruption and be without desire for reward.' The *Bhakti Rasāmṛit Sindhu* states:

anyābhilāşhitā-śhūnyaṁ jñāna-karmādy-anāvṛitam
ānukūlyena kṛişhṇānu-śhīlanaṁ bhaktir uttamā (1.1.11)

'Engage in devotion to the Supreme Lord with positive loving sentiments and without desire for material profit. Such devotion should be free from philosophic speculation and fruitive activities.'

Selfish Love Keeps Fluctuating

In material relationships, we often experience that our love for others keeps oscillating. The same father, mother, friend, teacher appear very endearing at one time. At other times, they appear normal, while at some other times, we start hating them. Our love for them does not remain steady.

The reason for this fluctuation is simply selfishness—we want something from them. When our self-interest is fulfilled, we think they are very nice. When our self-interest is not fulfilled, we feel they are just normal. And when our self-interest gets harmed, we dislike them. **If we love selflessly, then no matter how others behave with us, our love for them will not reduce.**

Similarly, if we love God selfishly, then our devotion towards Him will also keep fluctuating. Instead, if we learn selfless love, our devotion will steadily increase. The *Narad Bhakti Darshan* also states:

guṇarahitaṁ kāmanārahitaṁ pratikṣhaṇa vardhamānam
avichchhinnaṁ sūkṣhmataram anubhavarūpam (sutra 54)

'This love is beyond the three modes of material nature, above all desires, grows every moment, and remains incessant. It is subtler than the subtlest and is in the form of an experience.'

Seek God and All Else Will Be Added

Shree Krishna is the Supreme Master of unlimited universes. He possesses unimaginable treasures that He is eager to bestow upon the soul. Asking Him for material things is like meeting Kuber, the celestial god of wealth, and imploring him for a dollar. People would laugh in dismay and mock that person. Similarly, one who asks Shree Krishna for material things has no knowledge of the treasures of the divine realm.

A king once went to a foreign country. From there, he wrote to his queens asking them what they wanted. All the queens responded with expensive requests. The youngest queen simply wrote the number '1' in her letter to the king.

When the king returned, he brought the things that were requested by the other queens and instructed his servants to carry them to their respective rooms. But for the youngest queen, he personally went to her palace and asked, 'What was the meaning of the "1" you wrote? What did you want?'

The intelligent queen replied, 'The "1" meant I only wanted you, nothing else, and I got you. Thank you so much!'

Likewise, if we aspire for the world, we will not attain God. Conversely, if we make God our ultimate goal, we will automatically get His divine knowledge, love, and bliss. However, we must remember to love God and not do business with Him.

Difference between Business and Love

Business is a transactional activity characterized by give and take. We give to the other party with the intention of reciprocation or in anticipation of gain for ourselves. If we get more than what we gave, the business is considered profitable; else, the transaction is deemed unprofitable. Those engaged in business are inevitably concerned about what they stand to receive in return.

We often make the same mistake while engaging in devotion to God. We go to the temple and beseech the Lord for material boons. This is like doing business with Him. Suppose a trader says, 'Oh God! Give me five crores profit, and I will donate 50,000 rupees to the temple.' The trader is trying to engage God in a deal.

Selfless love is the stark opposite of business. In such love, we desire only to give...give...give without the expectation of reciprocation. Chaitanya Mahaprabhu expressed this very strongly:

kāmera tātparya nija-sambhoga kevala
kṛiṣhṇa-sukha-tātparya-mātra prema ta' prabala
ataeva kāma-preme bahuta antara
kāma—andha-tamaḥ, prema—nirmala bhāskara
(*Chaitanya Charitamrit, Ādi Leela*, 4.166 and 171)

'Where the desire is simply for self-happiness, that is lust; where the desire is desire for Lord Krishna's happiness, that is love. Lust is like darkness while love is pure like the Sun.'

Three Kinds of Seva

Real devotion is free from all self-seeking. However, to desire happiness is the nature of the soul. If selfless devotees do not want their own happiness, then what do they seek? **True devotees desire the happiness of God. They love Shree Krishna for His happiness alone. And to make Him happy, they wish to serve Him with everything they have.**

What can we give to God? We have three possessions with which we can serve Him:

1. **Mind.** Cultivate thoughts and sentiments that will make Shree Krishna happy.
2. **Body.** Engage the body in actions and service that are for the pleasure of God.
3. **Wealth.** Donate a portion of the income to causes that are pleasing to God.

Amongst these, serving with the mind is the most important, followed by the body, and finally, wealth. However, to reach the point where the mind remains engaged in loving thoughts, we must begin from below. We must learn to serve God with our wealth. Then we will develop the desire to engage the body in service as well. And when the body is engaged, the mind will naturally begin meditating on giving happiness to God.

This is why the scriptures instruct:

nyāyopārjita vittasya daśhamānśhena dhīmataḥ
kartavyo viniyogaśha cha īśhvaraprotyarthameva cha

(*Skanda Puran*)

'Whatever you have earned by genuine means, donate one-tenth in charity in the service of God. That is your duty.'

There are numerous benefits and advantages of donating one-tenth of one's income. It prevents one from misusing excessive wealth. It fosters a service attitude towards God. It expands the heart of the devotee. It teaches the devotee to practise selfless love. This principle in Hinduism is also practised in various other religions.

In the practice of *sadhana bhakti,* we will next discuss the need for meditation and its techniques.

18

The Art of Meditation

Meditation is a valuable contribution from Bharat to the world. It is known as 'dhyan' in Sanskrit. Its journey from Bharat to China led to modifications in its name, evolving from 'dhyan' to 'jhan,' and later to 'Zen,' which established itself as a prominent school of Mahayana Buddhism.

In the Western world, meditation remained relatively unknown until approximately 125 years ago. It was introduced by a wave of spiritual teachers who migrated from Bharat and imparted knowledge of the technique to Western audiences. Today, meditation has gained widespread recognition as a revered practice, finding its place in corporate boardrooms, fitness studios, universities, and wellness clinics.

The burgeoning popularity of meditation can be attributed to its numerous benefits, spanning the realms of physiology, psychology, and spirituality. Meditation serves as a powerful tool for calming the incessant stream of thoughts that inundate the mind, thereby fostering a sense of tranquillity. Through meditation, individuals can delve into the inner regions of their mind and intellect, for elevating their consciousness. One of the most notable advantages of meditation lies in its capacity to enhance the power of concentration.

Benefits of Concentration

At present, our mind is scattered in various directions. This not only diminishes our effectivity at work but also becomes a hindrance in devotion. We experience it when we sit to chant verses praising God, and the mind wanders in the world.

The untrained mind has been compared to a monkey. Saint Tulsidas says:

graha grahita puni bāt basa teahi puni bīchhī māra
tehi piāia bārunī kahahu kāha upachāra

(Ramayan, *Ayodhya Kand* 2.180)

'By nature, a monkey is restless. In addition, if it also has hysteria, how restless will it become. On top of that, if you make it drink alcohol, then consider its state. Further, if you tie a scorpion to its tail, then imagine the monkey's condition. Oh Lord! My mind is like that monkey.'

Concentration, on the other hand, enhances effectiveness. For example, water vapour rises from lakes and drifts ineffectively in the sky. Yet, when the same water vapour is concentrated in the form of steam and focussed on the piston of the railway engine, it becomes capable of propelling thousands of tons of carriages at the speed of hundreds of miles per hour. Similarly, an unwavering mind has tremendous power.

So, how can we enhance our concentration? We all have

experienced the challenges of restraining our wavering mind. Meditation offers a structured approach to train the mind to focus. A variety of meditation techniques can be used for this purpose.

Various Meditation Techniques

People practise meditation in many ways. Some meditate on the breath, while others fix their attention on the centre of the eyebrows, and yet others on the psychic centres in the spinal cord. Some choose to meditate on a tranquil lake, and others meditate on a light. All these different meditations do improve the focus of the mind. However, their benefits are incomplete and impermanent.

The drawback of these mechanical techniques is that the impurities in the mind do not get fully cleansed. As long as lust, anger, greed, envy, and illusion reside in the mind, these forces dissipate the concentration that was gained through practice.

The second problem is that these mechanical techniques aim at arresting the thought flow and bringing the mind to a void. This goes against the inherent nature of the mind, and hence, the practice of these techniques becomes uninteresting and difficult.

Advantages of Meditating upon God

Imagine you are riding a bicycle. If you apply the brakes, you will not be able to retain your balance. You will either topple to the left or to the right. However, if you gently steer the handle, the cycle will smoothly turn in the direction you desire. Similarly, the mind is a machine that continuously generates thoughts. If you try to stop the flow, it becomes an unstable condition, and such a thoughtless state is difficult to sustain. However, if you turn the mind towards God, it very easily begins meditating on the divine Names, Forms, Virtues, Abodes, and Pastimes of the Lord.

Meditation upon God is also very sweet. The mind, by nature, desires attractive forms, activities, sounds, and more. In devotion, the all-blissful Forms of God are a captivating subject matter for the mind to meditate upon.

Most importantly, God is all-pure, and when we fix our mind upon Him, it too becomes pure. The Bhagavad Gita states:

maṁ cha yo 'vyabhichāreṇa bhaktiyogena sevate
sa guṇān samatītyaitān brahma bhūyāya kalpate (14.26)

Shree Krishna tells Arjun: 'I am beyond the three modes of material nature. By engaging the mind in meditation upon Me, through bhakti yog, your mind will transcend the three modes and become divine.'

The Technique of Roop Dhyan Meditation

Roop Dhyan is meditation upon a Form of God. In this practice, we close our eyes and visualize the Lord before us or within our heart. Since the Form of God is naturally charming and attractive, the mind gets a wonderful subject upon which to focus. Consequently, the mind becomes steady with loving thoughts of God.

You may wonder how to bring the form of Radha Krishna to your mind when you have never seen Them. No need to worry. God is infinitely compassionate and allows you to imagine His form as you wish.

For instance, if you are drawn to the exquisite deities of Radha Krishna that you saw in some temple, you can make them the basis of your meditation. Attentively look at Them with your eyes open. Then close your eyes and try bringing Their image in front of you.

Alternatively, you can meditate on a beautiful picture of Radha Krishna. Or you may simply create Their image with your mind. In whatever way you choose to create Their Form, try to feel Their divine presence, and increase your love for Them.

If inclined, you can meditate solely on Shree Krishna or only on Radha Rani. Or if you prefer, you can bring the image of both Radha Krishna to your mind. Some people like to meditate exclusively on their Guru. That is fine as well. The key is to keep the mind in the divine realm. Ideally, you should first meditate on the Guru and receive his blessings, before proceeding to meditate on God.

Let us now learn of the different ways to meditate upon God.

The Technique of Meditating upon Divine Virtues

Our mind instinctively gravitates towards people's qualities. We say, 'This person is so kind-hearted', 'That woman is incredibly gentle', 'This boy is extremely intelligent', 'That girl is simply beautiful', and so on. Our mind's nature is to appreciate and dwell on the virtues of others. We can do the same in devotion. We can bring the unlimited divine qualities of Radha Krishna to our mind.

In this practice, first visualize the image of Radha Krishna before you. Then, ruminate over Their divine virtues:

- They are an ocean of mercy.
- They possess unlimited divine knowledge.
- They are so serene and peaceful.
- They are the veritable form of love.
- They are so beautiful.

Meditate upon the virtues of God and Guru. And then, visualize these qualities flowing from Them to you. In this manner, feel yourself becoming calm, content, knowledgeable, generous, loving, and happy. Similarly, perceive the grace of God flowing into your mind and body.

The Technique of Meditating upon Divine Pastimes

You can further immerse your mind in Radha Krishna by meditating upon Their divine Leelas. Factually, God has unlimited Pastimes. Each time He descends as an Avatar, He displays different Pastimes. And He has taken unlimited Avatars since eternity. The scriptures state:

nānā bhāñti rāma avatārā, rāmāyaṇa śhata koṭi apārā

(Ramayan, *Bal Kand* 1.32(B)-3)

hari ananta hari katha anantā

(Ramayan, *Bal Kand* 1.139.3)

The above verses state that Lord Ram descended in the material world innumerable times in countless ages. Each time He performed different Pastimes. Hence, there are innumerable Ramayanas in existence. Since God is unlimited, His Pastimes are also unlimited. Besides, in the divine Abodes of God, He keeps engaging in ever new Leelas at every moment. This is why you have the freedom to imagine His Leelas as you wish.

The Technique of Serving God in the Mind

Divine love is fundamentally rooted in the act of giving and finds expression in the desire to serve. Hence, devotees engage in various acts of service to the deities they worship. These include rituals such as bathing, clothing, adorning, and performing pooja (worship). However, all these and more can be performed in the mind as well through the technique of *mānasī* seva.

Mānasī seva is a simple and a deeply spiritual form of devotion. It is not restricted by traditional constraints associated with external rituals. Limitations that may hinder physical worship, such as the availability of flowers for offerings, are easily overcome in *mānasī* seva. Here, devotees envision and offer their service in their mind. Simply imagine offering a garland composed of the most exquisite roses, or visualize placing a bejewelled necklace more resplendent than the Kohinoor around Shree Krishna's neck.

Or perhaps, think Radha and Krishna are coming to your home, and you are welcoming Them with great love and respect. You can serve Them in various ways: wash Their feet, perform Their aarti, offer Them sumptuous food, and so on. If you wish to be more playful, you can even visualize yourself playing games like cricket or tennis with the Lord! In this manner, you can increase your love for Him.

Traveling with a physical deity can pose logistical challenges. Devotees often grapple with the dilemma of taking the deity along or leaving it behind. The latter option—leaving behind the deity without worship—can evoke a sense of discomfort in the devotee's heart. On the other hand, carrying the deity in check-in luggage presents its own set of complications, as it must be packed alongside shoes and undergarments, within the confines of baggage allowances imposed by airlines.

However, these concerns get resolved when we turn our focus to the power of visualization. By conjuring a mental image, we can engage in devotional practices at any time, without any physical requirements. In moments of free time, devotees can simply close their eyes and immerse themselves in serving the Lord—massaging His feet, offering food, and fanning Him, among other acts of devotion.

The primary benefit is that even more so than physical seva, *mānasī* seva serves to purify the mind. While it may appear straightforward, it facilitates practising noble thoughts, sacrifice, and service, all of which help cleanse the heart.

The Technique of Viraha Dhyan

This is meditation in the sentiment of longing for God. We do Roop Dhyan of Radha Krishna while harbouring the sentiment 'When will They give me actual darshan? The fact that They are not manifesting in person indicates that I still lack bhakti.' With a prayerful heart, the devotee then cries out for divine grace.

Viraha Dhyan is one of the deepest bhavs of meditation. What is the logic behind this? When our mind develops fondness for a person or an object, our senses find joy in it—the eyes want to see it, the tactile sense wants to feel it, and the ears want to hear its sounds. As it is said, 'Absence makes the heart grow fonder.'

For example, someone says, 'I have no other attachment in the world. But when I hear the broken words of my grandchild, I experience immense joy.' What does this statement imply? It implies that the person's mind is attached lovingly to his grandchild, making his childish gibberish pleasing to the ears.

Likewise, suppose your friend says, 'When I see rasagullas on the table, I begin salivating.' Why does this happen? Your friend's statement implies her mind is attached to rasagullas, and hence her tongue longs for their taste. By the same principle, when we develop love for God, our senses begin longing for Him. 'When will I see Shree Krishna?', 'When will I hear His divine flute?', 'When will I smell the flowers of His *vaijayanti* mala?', and so on.

In *Viraha Dhyan*, the goal is to proactively create this longing. It can include yearning for His divine darshan, for *para bhakti,* for divine seva of the *Iṣhṭa Dev*, and the like. The longing is accompanied by a humble awareness of the limitations of sadhana and need for God's grace. *Viraha Dhyan* is very intense. It is practised to enhance devotional yearning. Then, when one is tired, one can switch to meditation in union, through Roop Dhyan.

We have discussed a variety of meditative techniques. The next chapter shares insights on how to set up our daily sadhana and implement the various spiritual practices that have we have learnt through the chapters of this book.

19

How to Do Sadhana Daily

To progress in spirituality, we must do sadhana daily. Nobody can hope to become physically strong by exercising for five hours for simply one day. It is by consistently engaging in a fitness regimen that we become strong. Similarly, spiritual progress does not happen merely by doing devotion on Janmashtami and Ram Navami. This kind of half yearly bhakti will not bring the cherished results.

We must set up a daily schedule of bhakti. This regular practice will gradually and systematically lift our consciousness to God. It will increase our spiritual strength, just as daily exercises increase physical strength, and regular studying increases intellectual strength. There is a saying:

kśhaṇasaḥ kśhaṇasao vidya kānasaḥ kānaso dhanam

'By carefully saving a single dollar at a time, a person becomes a millionaire. By using each possible moment to study, one becomes a scholar.' Similarly, by engaging in sadhana daily, one attains divine love.

Where to Do Sadhana

We live in the material world and are constantly bombarded by its influences. An incessant stream of stimuli from the television, newspapers, and internet constantly tugs at our mind, taking it towards the world. In such an environment, it becomes difficult to think of God. This is why our daily sadhana must be done in seclusion where the world cannot disturb us.

The Bhagavad Gita instructs us to do such sadhana:

vivikta sevī laghv-āśhī (18.52)

'Practice in a secluded place; control your diet.'

Thus, isolate yourself from the world, while you practise meditation, contemplation, introspection, and devotion. If you have a worship room in your house, that is the best. Else, you can set aside a small corner of your home or your own bedroom for your devotional practice.

The place should be big enough for the altar and for the family members to sit. You must create a sacred environment in that place, so that when you sit there, the mind naturally gets transported to the divine realm.

What Direction to Face

There are no specifications regarding direction in bhakti meditation. The primary objective is to cleanse the mind of material impurities by absorbing it in the Supreme Divine Personality. Since the Lord is omnipresent, every direction is inherently pure. This fundamental concept of God's all-pervasiveness is emphasized throughout the Vedic scriptures:

purușha evedaṁ sarvaṁ yad bhūtaṁ yachcha bhāvyam

(*Purușha Sūktam* verse 2)

'God pervades everything that has existed and all that will exist.'

So, there is no necessity to dwell excessively on the correct or incorrect direction. Rather, our emphasis should be directed towards enriching our inner thoughts with sublime ideas.

What Posture to Adopt

The specific posture we choose is of secondary importance. Various meditative asanas (postures), such as padmasan, ardha padmasan, dhyānvīr asan, and siddhasan, are outlined in the *Haṭha Yog Pradīpikā*. We may comfortably select any posture for meditation—one in which we can remain still during meditation. Maharishi Patanjali, the proponent of Ashtang Yog, emphasized *sthira sukhamāsanam* (2.46) 'To practise meditation, sit motionless in any posture that you find comfortable.'

Regardless of the chosen posture, try to maintain an alert and upright position during meditation. In the practice of sadhana, there is a tendency for the mind to resist divine contemplation, leading to a sense of lethargy. Consequently, you may find yourself dozing off during meditation. To counter this tendency, maintaining an upright posture is crucial.

The *Brahma Sutra* (*Vedant Darshan*) has three aphorisms on the topic of sadhana:

āsīnaḥ saṁbhavāt (4.1.7)
'To do sadhana, seat yourself properly.'

achalatvaṁ chāpekṣhya (4.1.9)
'Ensure that you sit upright and still.'

dhyānāchcha (4.1.8)
'Seated in this manner, focus the mind in meditation.'

If you have knee problems or joint pains, you need not be disheartened. You can engage in your meditative practice even while seated on a chair.

The Principle Behind Deity Worship

If you were asked to love a white light, you would find it almost impossible since the mind would not be drawn to it. Our mind is naturally attracted to forms and shapes. When the Lord's image is in front of us, it becomes easier to think of Him and love Him. This is why deity worship is practised in Hindu temples around the world.

Deities are made from stone, wood, metal, and other materials. These deities are installed with great faith and devotion. The Lord is then requested to manifest in that deity, to receive the devotees' offerings. God is present everywhere, so why would He not be present in His deity?

What connects us with God is not the idol itself, but the bhav that we harbour. The *Manu Smriti* states:

na kāṣhṭhe vidyate devo na śhilayāṁ na mṛitsu cha
bhāve hi vidyate devastasmāt bhāvaṁ samācharet

'The bhav we harbour towards the deity is important, not the stone or mud. God is present wherever the bhav is present. Therefore, worship the idol with great bhav.'

More importantly, we get to practise devotion. This is just as astronauts, before being sent into space, practise how to live in zero-gravity environments in a simulator. Likewise, we will serve God in person after going to His divine Abode. In the interim, we get to simulate the seva with the deity.

However, deity worship has many rigorous rules that must be adhered to. It is suitable for the temple, but for your own home, it is cumbersome because of the regulations. Instead, there is a simpler option. You can choose to visualize the Form of the Lord with your mind and make it the object of your meditation and devotion, as discussed in the previous chapter.

Integrating Contemplation, Meditation, and Devotion in Your Sadhana

Having broadly discussed the importance and logistics of sadhana, we can now get into its details. Below is an outline of the different techniques we can include in our sadhana.

Preparation for Sadhana

1. Create an altar adorned with images of God and Guru, and then sit before it. This external arrangement fosters an environment conducive to devotional absorption. It is important to note that this step is optional; if preferred, you can meditate without external props. For instance, you may choose to commence your meditation upon waking by sitting upright on your bed.
2. Assume a comfortable seated posture, as elaborated earlier in the chapter.

3. Initiate your sadhana by visualizing the image of God before you.

After step three, with the divine Form before you, you are now ready to engage in sadhana. Below are various spiritual practices that you can incorporate, which we have discussed earlier in this book.

Spiritual Practice 1

Do Roop Dhyan meditation. Envision an image of God and/or your Guru within your heart or before you. This provides the mind with a tangible focal point for concentration. This has been explained in detail in Chapter 18: The Art of Meditation, in the section, 'The Technique of Roop Dhyan Meditation'.

Spiritual Practice 2

Contemplate upon the wonderful divine virtues of God. This will help enchant your mind towards the Lord and intensify your connection with Him. This has been explained in detail in Chapter 18: The Art of Meditation, in the section, 'The Technique of Meditating upon Divine Virtues'.

Spiritual Practice 3

Repeatedly think about your eternal relationship with God, deepening your love for Him. Think and repeatedly affirm: *He is mine and I am His*. This has been explained in detail in Chapter 16: Sadhana Bhakti—Preparatory Devotion, in the sections, 'Our Eternal Relationship with God' and 'The Need to Rekindle Our Relationship'.

Spiritual Practice 4

Cultivate the spirit of surrender in the mind through self-talk. For example, repeatedly think, *I must align my desire with God's desire. I must not desire anything contrary to His will.* This has been explained in detail in Chapter 8: Surrender to God, in the section, 'Nature of Sharanagati'.

Spiritual Practice 5

Nurture selfless love by serving God in the mind. Such service will give rise to contemplation upon His happiness instead of your own. It will develop the habit of giving rather than receiving. This has been explained in detail in Chapter 18: The Art of Meditation, in the section, 'The Technique of Serving God in the Mind'.

Spiritual Practice 6

Contemplate. Take any gem of wisdom you found in this book and internalize it through contemplation. This has been explained in detail in Chapter 10: Vedic Psychology, in the section, 'The Impact of Repetitive Thinking'.

Spiritual Practice 7

Increase your longing to meet God. Pray to Him with wholehearted sincerity. Allow tears to flow as you earnestly seek His grace. Cultivate a profound yearning for His darshan while embracing the virtue of utmost humility. This has been explained in detail in Chapter 18: The Art of Meditation, in the section, 'The Technique of Roop Dhyan Meditation'.

Spiritual Practice 8

Feel the presence of God. Following your daily sadhana—as outlined above—practise feeling the presence of God for the rest of the day. This will enable you to fulfil your worldly responsibilities while maintaining a devout connection with the Divine. This has been explained in detail in Chapter 11: The Path of Karm, in the section, 'Karm Yog—Uniting with the Supreme through Action'.

You have the option to incorporate any or all of these powerful techniques mentioned above into your daily spiritual routine, either individually or in combination.

While these methods are straightforward, some newcomers may find them challenging. If you seek a simpler approach, consider the practice of kirtan (chanting).

The Importance of Kirtan

Kirtan is the most powerful way to bring divine thoughts to your mind. It involves three activities: (1) Chanting prayers and the Names, Virtues, Leelas of God in melodious tunes. (2) Hearing the chants with your ears. (3) Absorbing your mind in the Divine.

Kirtan is the combination of all these activities, and hence it is also called *tridhā bhakti* (three-fold devotion). This kirtan is called the *yuga dharma*, or the most powerful spiritual practice of this age and is accessible to everyone. Chanting and hearing are important aids to remembering God. The Shreemad Bhagavatam states:

kalerdoṣhanidhe rājannasti hyeko mahān guṇaḥ
kīrtanād eva kṛiṣhṇasya muktasaṅgaḥ paraṁ vrajet
(verse 12.3.51)

This verse states that Kali Yug, the present era, is an ocean of faults. People have disturbed minds, unsound health, polluted environment, and face disturbing situations. However, it has one very great advantage. By lovingly singing melodious kirtans, one can easily get liberated from material bondage.

The Daily Routine

The optimal time for doing bhakti is during the morning hours. When you wake up, your mind is vacant. It is receptive to focussing on God. Additionally, the morning atmosphere is fresh and calm, making it conducive for elevating the mind. However, it is not compulsory to engage in devotional practice only in the morning. If busy with other engagements, then do your sadhana in the afternoon, evening, or even at night, depending upon your convenience. The key is to establish a consistent routine by adhering to the same time every day. This will help in disciplining the mind.

How much time should we spend on devotion? Ideally, we must aim for two hours of sadhana every day. We spend 24 hours a day taking care of the body and its desires. The injunction of the scriptures is to keep one-tenth for God. Nowadays, people find it difficult to dedicate two hours from their busy schedules. So, I suggest committing a minimum of one hour for this practice.

A suggested sequence of what to do for the one hour is given below. I call this the '**KripaluPadhati**':

Prathana (5 minutes). Say a daily prayer at the altar.

Roop Dhyan Meditation (15 minutes). Meditate on God and your Guru for 15 minutes.

Kirtan (15 minutes). Sing or listen to kirtans with a deep feeling that God and His Names are non-different. Alongside, visualize the presence of God and Guru before you.

Listen to a Lecture (20 minutes). Spend time listening to a divine discourse or reading scriptures to cultivate knowledge and enhance your faith in God and Guru.

Aarti (5 minutes). Light up a lamp and do aarti to end the daily sadhana.

Conclusion

When we apply ourselves to the various spiritual practices described above, the yearning to meet Radha Krishna will start growing. This will purify our mind even further. And that will increase the longing even more, which will further cleanse the mind. This cascading effect will result in an intense yearning for darshan, prem, and seva. This yearning of the heart is called *viraha*. It will grow so deep that it will burn away all remaining impurities. A stage will arrive when the entire world will appear void without God. Chaitanya Mahaprabhu described this in His *Shikshastakam*:

yugāyitaṁ nimeṣhena chakṣhuṣhā prāvṛaṣhāyitam
śhunyāyitaṁ jagat sarvaṁ govinda-viraheṇa me (verse 7)

'In longing for Shree Krishna, a single moment is appearing an age long; tears are constantly streaming from the eyes; and the whole world is appearing void.'

At that stage, our heart will be pure. With our mind fully attached to God, we will be at the stage of: *mām ekaṁ śharaṇaṁ vraja*. Having fulfilled His condition for grace, we will receive *para bhakti*. The Vedas state:

bhidyate hṛidayagranthiśhchhidyante sarvasaṅśhayāḥ
kṣhīyante chāsya karmāṇi tasmindṛiṣhṭe parāvare (2.2.8)

This verse from the Mundakopanishad explains that the moment we receive divine love, the bondage of maya will immediately cease. The *sañchit* karmas of all past lives will be burnt, all doubts will be cut asunder, and we will have darshan of God. From then on, our soul will be endowed with God's unlimited divine love, bliss, and knowledge. It is then that we will become *jivan mukta*, or liberated even while in the body.

When we leave our body at the end of our life, we will go to the divine Abode of God. There, we will receive a divine body and serve Him in His eternal Pastimes. This is the ultimate goal and purpose of life.

Glossary

ahāṅkār	ego
ajnana	lack of knowledge, ignorance
antaḥ karaṇ	ethereal heart
atma	soul
atma jnana	self-realization or knowledge of the self (soul)
Bhagavan	personal form of God
Brahma jnana	God-realization or knowledge of God
Brahman	formless aspect of God
brahmanand	bliss of the formless aspect of God
chitta	subconscious mind
darshan	to see/view
devatas (*devatās*)	celestial gods
gadā	mace
Golok	divine abode of Shree Krishna
Hlādini shakti	bliss giving aspect of Yogmaya
Iṣhṭa Dev	chosen form of God for worship
jiva (*jīva*)	individual soul

kām	lust
Kailash	divine abode of Lord Shiv
kāmanā	desire
karm kāṇḍ	ritualistic ceremonies prescribed by the scriptures
kriyamāṇ karma	actions we do in the present by our own free will
leelas	divine pastimes of God and His associates
mānas rog	mental illnesses
mānasī seva	to serve God in the mind
maya	God's insentient, material energy
mithya	non-existent
mṛiga tṛiṣhṇā	illusion, mirage seen by the deer
namaste	the Hindu way of greeting the other with respect and humility
niṣhkām bhakti	selfless devotion
nitya leela	eternal pastimes of the Lord
Paramatma	aspect of God seated within all living beings
parikrama	to circumambulate a deity or a place of worship
prārabdh karma	portion of sanchit karmas that we have to face in the present life
prasad	food that has been offered to God as is partaken as His leftovers
premanand	bliss of the personal form of God

Roop Dhyan	meditation done while focusing on the Form of God
sadhaks (*sādhaks*)	spiritual aspirants
sadhana	spiritual practice
sadhana bhakti	devotion we have to engage in to purify the mind
sakām bhakti	devotion tinged with selfishness
Saket Lok	divine abode of Shree Ram
samadhi	state of deep meditation
sanatan	eternal
sañchit karma	all the accumulated karmas that we performed in endless past lives
sanskars (*sanskārs*)	tendencies from previous lifetimes
Sarva-śhaktimān	He who possesses unlimited energies
seva	service; to serve
Shaktimãn	Energetic, source of energies
śharaṇãgat	one who is surrendered
śharaṇãgati	surrender
shastras	scriptures
siddha bhakti	divine love bestowed by God once our mind is pure
Smṛiti	knowledge revealed in the hearts of Saints who then documented it as texts
swarg	celestial abodes
tattva darśhi	Seer of Truth
Tretã Yug	second in the cycle of four yugas (ages)

	as per the Vedic scriptures
tridhā bhakti	three-fold devotion
upāsanā	to get close to God
upavās	to fast
Vaikunth	divine abode of Lord Vishnu
Varnashram Dharma	duties prescribed by the scriptures based on one's stage in life (age) and occupation (personality)
Viraha Dhyan	meditation done while visualizing the longing to meet God
yajnas	fire sacrifices
Yogmaya	God's personal power, in contrast to maya, His external and insentient energy

Guide to Hindi Pronunciation

Vowels

अ	*a*	as *u* in 'but'
आ	*ā*	as *a* in 'far'
इ	*i*	as *i* in 'pin'
ई	*ī*	as *i* in 'machine'
उ	*u*	as *u* in 'push'
ऊ	*ū*	as *o* in 'move'
ए	*e*	as *a* in 'evade'
ऐ	*ai*	as *a* in 'mat'; sometimes as *ai* in 'aisle' with the only difference that *a* should be pronounced as *u* in 'but', not as *a* in 'far'
ओ	*o*	as *o* in 'go'
औ	*au*	as *o* in 'pot' or as *aw* in 'saw'
ऋ	*ṛi*	as *ri* in 'Krishna'[17]
ॠ	*ṛī*	as *ree* in 'spree'

[17]Across the many states of India, *ṛi* is pronounced as *ru* as *u* in p*u*sh. In most parts of North India, *ṛi* is pronounced as *ri* in K*ri*shna. We have used the North Indian style here.

Consonants

Gutturals: Pronounced from the throat

क	*ka*	as *k* in 'kite'
ख	*kha*	as *kh* in 'Eckhart'
ग	*ga*	as *g* in 'goat'
घ	*gha*	as *gh* in 'dighard'
ङ	*ṅa*	as *n* in 'finger'

Palatals: Pronounced with the middle of the tongue against the palate

च	*cha*	as *ch* in 'channel'
छ	*chha*	as *chh* in 'staunchheart'
ज	*ja*	as *j* in 'jar'
झ	*jha*	as *dgeh* in 'hedgehog'
ञ	*ña*	as *n* in 'lunch'

Cerebrals: Pronounced with the tip of the tongue against the palate

ट	*ta*	as *t* in 'tub'
ठ	*ṭha*	as *th* in 'hothead'
ड	*ḍa*	as *d* in 'divine'
ढ	*ḍha*	as *dh* in 'redhead'
ण	*ṇa*	as *n* in 'burnt'

Dentals: Pronounced like the cerebrals but with the tongue against the teeth

त	ta	as *t* in the French word 'matron'
थ	tha	as *th* in 'ether'

द	da	as *th* in 'either'
ध	dha	as *dh* in 'Buddha'
न	na	as *n* in 'no'

Labials: Pronounced with the lips

प	*pa*	as *p* in 'pink'
फ	*pha*	as *ph* in 'uphill'
ब	*ba*	as *b* in 'boy'
भ	*bha*	as *bh* in 'abhor'
म	*ma*	as *m* in 'man'

Semivowels

य	*ya*	as *y* in 'yes'
र	*ra*	as *r* in 'remember'
ल	*la*	as *l* in 'light'
व	*va*	as *v* in 'vine', as *w* in 'swan'

Sibilants

श	*śha*	as *sh* in 'shape'
ष	*ṣha*	as *sh* in 'show'
स	*sa*	as *s* in 'sin'

Aspirate

ह	*ha*	as *h* in 'hut'

Visarga

:	*ḥ*	it is a strong aspirate; also lengthens the preceding vowel and occurs only at the end of a word. It is pronounced as a final *h* sound

Anusvara Nasalized

ं	ṁ/ṅ	nasalizes and lengthens the preceding vowel and is pronounced as *n* in the words 'and' or 'anthem'[18]
ँ	~	as *n* in 'gung-ho'

Avagraha

ऽ	*Ó*	This is a silent character indicating अ. It is written but not pronounced; used in specific combination (sandhi) rules

Others

क्ष	*kṣha*	as *ksh* in 'freakshow'
ज्ञ	*jña*	as *gy* in 'bigyoung'
ड़	*ṛa*	There is no sign in English to represent the sound ड़. It has been written as *ṛa*, but the tip of the tongue quickly flaps down
ढ़	*ṛha*	There is no sign in English to represent the sound ढ़. It has been written as *ṛha*, but the tip of the tongue quickly flaps down
ज़	*z*	as *z* in the word 'zaroor'

[18]Sometimes nasalized and sometimes not. In many words such as *Aṁsh*, *Saṁskar*, etc. are pronounced with a nasal sound as *Aṅsh*, *Saṅskar*, etc. Since it is nasalized, we are using *ṅ*.

Let's Connect

If you enjoyed reading this book and would like to connect with Swami Mukundananda, you can reach him through any of the following channels:

Websites: *www.jkyog.org, www.jkyog.in, www.swamimukundananda.org*

YouTube channels: 'Swami Mukundananda' and 'Swami Mukundananda Hindi'

Facebook: 'Swami Mukundananda' and 'Swami Mukundananda Hindi'

Instagram: 'Swami Mukundananda' and 'Swami Mukundananda Hindi'

Pinterest: Swami Mukundananda – JKYog

Telegram: Swami Mukundananda

Twitter: Swami Mukundananda (@Sw_Mukundananda)

LinkedIn: Swami Mukundananda

Podcasts: Apple, Google, SoundCloud, Spotify, Stitcher

JKYog Radio: TuneIn app for iOS and Android

JKYog App: Available for iOS and Android

WhatsApp Daily Inspirations: We have two broadcast lists. You are welcome to join either or both.

India: +91 84489 41008
USA: +1 346-239-9675

Online Classes:

JKYog India: *www.jkyog.in/online-sessions/*
JKYog US: *www.jkyog.org/online-classes*

Email: deskofswamiji@swamimukundananda.org

To bring *Spiritual Secrets from Hinduism* or Swami Mukundananda to your organization—as Google, Intel, Oracle, Verizon, United Nations, Stanford University, Yale University, IITs and IIMs have done—look us up at *sm-leadership.org*.